Rose Hill to Roundhill: a Brighton Community

Dedicated to the memory of Lindsey Lee, a member of the Roundhill Local History Group

contents:

Published in 2004 by Brighton Books Publishing

Cover: 'Brighton. A Bird's Eye View from Round Hill' by J Cordwell 1819
Inside front cover: looking up the cat creep in summer
Previous page: entrance doorway to Fern Villa
Opposite page: looking down the cat creep in winter

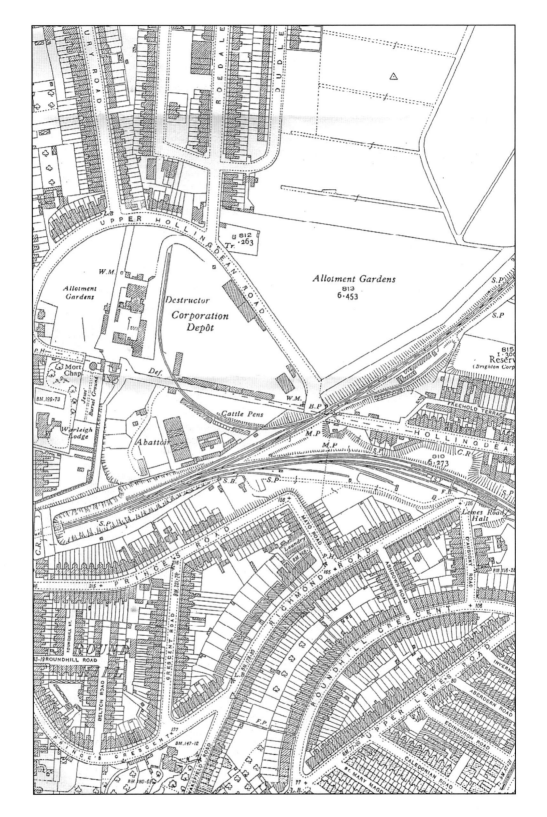

4

Foreword

Roundhill is really a triangle. Something magical happens when you put three crosses on the map and begin to join the dots. An old faded picture comes into view. This book is a timeline guide to that picture.

Bringing together over two hundred years of history, this is the story of the sights and sounds, the people and their occupations and pre-occupations, who all lived, worked and weaved their lives in a special part of Brighton.

From children playing in the cat creep through to artisans varnishing window sashes, from Victorian entrepreneurs founding factories to railway workers bringing new life to the locality, this is the hidden history of an area that represents a slice through time that is utterly individual.

Pull up a pew and sprinkle these magic dots over the pages. 'Rosehill to Roundhill: A Brighton Community' is a journey down overgrown archways into a world beneath your feet.

Hold this book and watch it catch the light, like a jewel with three roughly weathered edges, what you will see, crystallised, is some of the magic of Brighton itself.

Opposite: 1931 map of Roundhill

Below: Roundhill from Tenantry Down 2003, terraces built following the contours of the hill as in Georgian Bath

Introduction

In 1800 the steep 200 foot, rounded hill to the north of fashionable Brighton was arable farmland crossed by chalk paths connecting Preston village with the road to Lewes. Round Hill was owned by several landowners including Thomas Kemp, and William Stanford, whose family had bought it as part of a swathe of land which encircled Brighton and Hove. The Stanfords were soon to turn from farming to property development on a large scale, transforming agricultural Round Hill to the Roundhill we know now.

Travelling along Upper Lewes Road today you are likely to have to contend with traffic congestion and pollution, but one hundred and fifty years ago a different view would have greeted you. An engraving of 1778 shows a prominent downland hill with faintly defined footpaths. An 1819 print shows crops being gathered from the hillside looking down to the Level (see cover)

In 1823 the lower part of the hill was turned into Ireland's, or the Royal, Pleasure Gardens. They included a cricket ground, a maze, an aviary and a small lake. This proved an unsuccessful venture and by the 1840s the land had been sold for the development of Park Crescent.

Before long Round Hill's summit was crowned by Tower Mill, and at its foot paired villas appeared in Ditchling Road. At the back of the hill ran a track known as Dog Kennel Road, because the kennels of the Brighton Harriers were located there. The Parish Dust Yard soon joined the Kennels and later the Municipal Abattoir, making this northern side of the hill the home of a number of less appealing aspects of town life.

Meanwhile the sunny southern slope was developed from the first villas in Ditchling Road into the curving streets that follow the contour of the hill, providing a surprising view of Brighton from the Race Hill (see page 5). That took place between 1865 and 1880, but it left many sizeable pockets of land which became thriving nurseries and small holdings, several of which survived until the 1950s. The distance from the centre of the town, the height above it and the space also provided the impetus for the growth of many laundries, which needed breezy, open areas as drying grounds.

When the railway came in the middle of the 19th century it formed a partial barrier between the southern and the northern sides. As local stations were

Opposite: view of Brighton from Rose Hill North c1845

built along the line in the 1880s many railway employees moved in changing the social mix. As the area grew a few industries moved in to tap the supply of workers, though only one – the Cox's Pill Factory – was on a substantial scale. The others were much smaller, ranging from fly proprietors, builders and craftsmen's yards and laundries, to the Fisher Golf Ball factory.

Today Roundhill is almost entirely residential, save for the Council yard. It has a thriving Community Association and as a Conservation Area it is conscious of its inheritance.

This book traces the development of this unique triangular area of high land and the social life of its inhabitants as they went to school, worked, shopped, survived medical epidemics, lived through bombing, went for a drink in local pubs,.visited the cinema and met their friends,

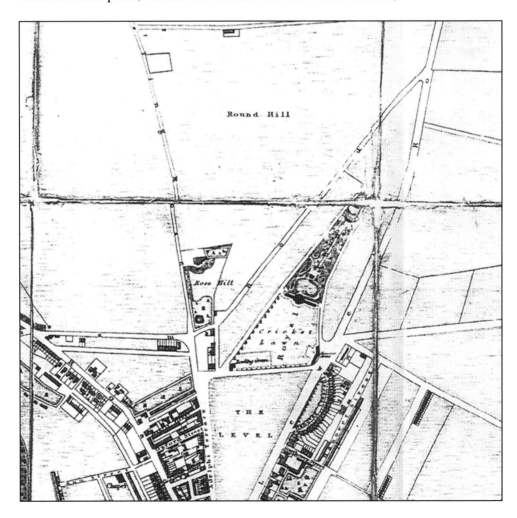

One: Early Roundhill

One of the most interesting aspects of the history of the area is the diversity of life within its boundaries. Two totally different focal points marked the early history of the area, which are largely unknown today.

As well as marking the home of a hunting pack back in the 19th century, the Roundhill map also indicates a burial ground. What joins these two points together is not just their position, it is the name of one man, Thomas Kemp.

The Brighton Harriers

Brighton once had its own hunting Harrier pack founded in 1761. Originally the kennels were situated in the old chalk pit that used to exist between Regent Row and Upper North Street, roughly where the Benefit Office presently stands. In 1811 the kennels were moved to Preston Circus on the site of the Duke of York's cinema..

In the 1850s Thomas Read Kemp donated a site in Hollingdean Road for the building of a house and kennels. The condition of the gift being

'that it should belong exclusively to the Brighton Hunt'.

The hounds of the Brighton Harriers were kennelled there from the 1850s to the 1870s. The Ordnance Survey map of 1875 showed the kennels abutting Hollingdean Road just below the Jewish cemetery. The Harriers met every Monday, Wednesday and Saturday at 11 o'clock during the season, until near the end of the nineteenth century.

Opposite: 1830 map of the Round Hill area, with Rose Hill, the Cricket Lawn, the Level, Hanover Crescent, with buildings on part of the North Butts open field, or laine, to the west of The Level

Jewish Burial Ground

One of the most unusual and least known features of Roundhill is the Jewish Burial Ground in Florence Place, hidden behind 'The Jolly Brewer' public house.

In 1826, Thomas Kemp, local Member of Parliament and founder of Kemp Town, donated a small piece of land to the congregation of the Brighton Synagogue for use as their burial ground. The land was separated from the town at the rear by open fields. Crops surrounded the burial ground on three sides and on the northern side was the Brighton Parish dustyard, which had been in operation since 1810. Thomas Kemp probably felt that this site would not be popular with potential buyers and therefore would cost him less to donate than other possible sites in the town.

A red brick octagonal mortuary chapel with a turret roof, the Ohel, a Grade II listed building, designed by Lainson & Son in 1893, still stands today and is the only part of the burial ground that can be clearly seen by looking east from Ditchling Road by the 'Jolly Brewer' public house. Some funerals are still conducted on this site and the hand washing facility at the rear of the chapel is still used. It is a tradition for Jewish people to wash their hands on leaving the presence of death. The normal custom for symbolic washing of hands after visiting a cemetery is to use a two handled container to pour water over each hand in turn.

> '. . . previous burials [were] in London. To raise funds for enclosing the ground and erecting the 'Ohel' a tax of 2 shillings per week per member for one year was imposed on the Congregation. Levi Emmanuel Cohen and Mr Berncastle lent £50 interest free and Moses Mocatta £25 - but only for four months . . Problems arose over the guarding of the cemetery during the period of 'body-snatching'. Records show that a bathing machine was used as a sort of 'guard room' for those maintaining watch.'
> **The Jews of Brighton – The Jewish Historical Society of England Transactions – Sessions 1968-1969 volume XXII.**

The tightly packed gravestones in the Jewish cemetery reveal a part of Brighton's early history. One of the most interesting gravestones is that of the Chief Constable of Brighton, Henry Solomon, murdered on 14 March 1844, by a deranged youth named John Lawrence. Lawrence struck the Chief Constable with a poker and Solomon died the next day leaving a widow and nine children. John Lawrence was swiftly tried and publicly

Opposite: the red brick octagonal mortuary chapel with a turret roof, the Ohel

hung at Horsham less than a month after the murder. A public appeal raised a large sum for the widow, and the Brighton Commissioners gave £500.

Other remarkable people buried in the cemetery are Hyam Lewis and Emmanuel Cohen. The first was the Brighton Town Commissioner in the 1830s (roughly equivalent to an elected mayor today), the first recorded Jew to hold municipal office in the entire country. He paid for the tombstone of Phoebe Hessel in St Nicholas churchyard. The Lewis family continued to provide councillors for the town until 1955, and one well known descendent was Lord Lewis Cohen of Brighton. The other, Emmanuel Cohen, was the firebrand editor of the 'Brighton Guardian' in the 1840s, a newspaper he founded. Cohen got into deep trouble for some mild criticism of the intelligence of William IV in 1830, and was hounded repeatedly by the Tory magistrates of the town for his radically Liberal views. He spent time in Chelmsford gaol on trumped up charges but continued writing his damning editorials under he heading 'from Chelmsford gaol'. Not a man to harbour grudges Cohen was later instrumental in getting a charter for Brighton as a Municipal Borough.

Originally a gardener, who lived on the premises, was employed to look after the graveyard, but the cemetery is now overgrown and locked to secure the safety of the tombstones, many with Hebrew inscriptions. The crowded burial ground is rarely used now because the small piece of land has become inadequate for the needs of the Jewish community, except where a space in a family grave is available. An alternative site has been provided at the top of Bear Road. A memorial stone to commemorate the opening of the burial ground remains embedded in the surrounding wall.

Two: Victorian Roundhill

If ever a model were to be needed to demonstrate much of the rich architectural history of Brighton the model makers could do little better than concentrate on Roundhill, for within its acres are good examples of much that is best about Brighton's buildings and layers of philanthropy and foppery.

From curving crescents to villas, workmen's yards, schools, factories, hidden architectural gems and Victorian estates, the area has it all. Every building in the Roundhill area has its own story to tell, joined together the omnibus edition reads like book of Brighton's architectural history.

Bricks and Mortar

Round Hill covers almost the whole gamut of Brighton buildings, from the majestic sweep of Round Hill Crescent to the low cottages on Ditchling Road beside the 'Jolly Brewer' public house. The area saw four spacious mansions built, a number of delightful villas and a flood of classic Victorian bay-fronted houses.

Like so much of Brighton the area is not quite what it seems. Good quality facing brick was expensive in the 19th century so builders used poor quality brick, even a rubble known locally as 'bungaroosh', and covered it with cement render as protection against the marine climate. A hundred and thirty years later we can say it worked well. A few buildings were of traditional flint, of which some survive in Princes Road; others used to be in Upper Lewes Road and Roundhill Crescent.

Wooden framed sash windows were universal, along with slate roofs. Many of the window frames are now plastic, and almost all the roofs are of concrete tile. The pavements originally would have been only compacted earth, but in a few places blue brick pavers were used, some of which still survive in Mayo Road.

Development started in 1840 with the construction of the four fine mansions in the secluded grounds on what is today the Sylvan Hall Estate. Around 1865 fine curving terraces of Regency style houses with iron balconies appeared at either end of Round Hill Crescent, whilst further up the hill the more modest villas which today line one side of Richmond Road were erected.

After a slight pause building work again took off around 1880 with the rest of Round Hill Crescent being erected in the typical bay-fronted style of the period. As elsewhere on the Stanford Estate, the lots were developed by small builders to their own design within a broad general plan laid down by the Estate and as dictated by the fall of the land. Thus some are three storeys but most two. In this style the streets of Princes, Ashdown, D'Aubigny, Mayo, Wakefield and Lennox, etc. were set out. The last named never achieved that status as it was felt too steep for horses to go up and instead became a cat creep.

After this growth the area was steadily infilled: some houses around 1914, some in the 20s and again in the 60s, and some more houses were built as recently as 2003 on land at the lower end of Belton Road.

Within this broad picture there are a number of particularly interesting houses. These include two in D'Aubigny Road which stand out as of different style. There is the substantial brick house that was built for Arthur Cox of pill factory fame, and the double fronted local Stationmaster's house at the top of the road on the other side. Both these bring a sense of character to an otherwise rather modest street.

Standing at the top of Islingword Road and looking across the valley towards Roundhill the eye is caught by a solitary white house, built in 1878, in the midst of the curving terraces. Curiosity will take you to a hidden gem, reached through a low doorway between 13 and 15 Wakefield Road. The name 'Fern Villa' is written over the arch (see photograph on first page).

A recent occupant described life at Fern Villa in the 1940s.

"When my family moved into number 14 in early 1939 the garden was beautiful with lawns on both sides of the path, with flowers and shrubs and some trees against the wall below the other houses. I can clearly remember the trees because I used to climb up to numbers 16 & 18 to visit girl friends. Then everyone 'Dug for Victory' and the whole garden became a vegetable plot. After the war it was never the same. The sunken garden however, was left untouched, with a central patch of lawn bordered by flowerbeds including a small hedge of loganberries. Besides the greenhouse were two small apple trees which bore masses of fruit. My grandmother made sure we had plenty of apple and berry pies. The greenhouse was my grandfather's domain, despite the fact he only had one leg and moved around on a wooden kitchen chair. He produced copious amounts of tomatoes and

lettuce. We ate well in those days! 14 Wakefield Road, my home from 1939 to 1953, was a source of great happiness throughout the war years. Despite the dangers from an odd bomb the house resounded with laughter.'
Colin Mather

Another particularly interesting house is Princes Villa, which on an 1867 map stood alone at the high point of Crescent Road and Princes Road. An 1873 map of central Brighton shows a detached house fronting onto Crescent Road, surrounded by large, well laid out gardens and a stable. The stable yard entrance was in Princes Road. The house still stands today, the only clue to its age being the old, brick-patched, flint wall that curves around the corner.

It was built in 1866 by James Stapleton, an 'eating house keeper' of North Road, who purchased the land from the Round Hill Park Estate, which had originally belonged to Thomas Read Kemp. At first his eldest son James Hasler Stapleton lived there with his family, but later his parents moved in and stayed there until the death of James senior in 1892.

The house was left to the two surviving sons. One, Charles Edward Stapleton, was a jeweller in Black Lion Street whilst Alfred, his brother, was the licensee of the 'Victory Inn' in Duke Street. According to the terms of the will

> 'the net rents and annual proceeds of the property must be paid to their mother, Jane, during her life'

and after her death they were to

> 'sell and absolutely dispose of the property'.

Hence in 1895 Princes Villa was sold to William Bennett, a stonemason of 119 Lewes Road. He owned it for about thirty years but never lived there himself. Around the turn of the century it became the Victoria Laundry, one of the many in the area, with stabling and a large piece of adjacent land for drying. (see Laundries chapter). The laundry changed hands three times in four years, so business may not have been good.

When William Bennett died in 1924 his family began to sell off parts of the garden as building plots, and four houses were built on the land. Princes Villa itself was then sold and the new owner converted it into two dwellings to rent. In 1939 it was on the market again and was purchased by the Love family, who kept it for over 20 years but allowed it to fall into disrepair. In 1956 the Council ordered 'the south basement room to be closed for all purposes'. After passing through other hands and being divided into four flats a fire caused extensive damage in the mid 80s.

"It was about 5 pm. My partner smelled smoke and we thought it might be a bonfire somewhere. I went into the children's playroom and looked out of the window. I saw somebody in Crescent Road pointing up at the roof to me. We both opened the door into the roof space and smoke came pouring out. It was OK because we had insurance and the place was completely rebuilt, but we were homeless for six months."
Lynn Mansfield-Osbourne

"I heard lots of people in the road and went out to see what was going on. It was dark. Outside most of the houses were people talking and shouting. It was shocking; the flames leaping out of the roof with smoke billowing. I knew the occupants and didn't know whether they were in there!'
Christine Zaniewicka

In the 1920s, after the new houses had been built in what had been the garden of the Villa, the stable block became 36a Princes Road. In its time it has housed a number of commercial enterprises. In 1930 it was the home to Franklin and Son, a wholesale haberdasher. At the beginning of World War Two it was a garage and then, up until 1971, it was Johnson's Joinery Works where cuckoo clocks were made. For a short time Hydrift Precision Engineering used it, but the Council closed it down after reports of oil running down Princes Road. The next occupant was Zebra Brakes and they remained there until 1983. It is now Floline Trading, heating and plumbing trade suppliers.

Another early building that stands out is Hill House, 50 Princes Road, but dating only from 1878. Current owners Jenn and Marigold explain its history.

"We bought 50 Princes Road in 1993, fascinated by its unusual appearance - flint walls, brick quoins and gables, ornate barge boards, a sizable garden and a spacious, dry cellar with a large Belfast sink. We managed to find the original 'Plans for a proposed Cottage on Round Hill Estate, Plot 321 in Princes Road', dated 1875. These show a large front parlour, a kitchen and scullery at the back, two upstairs bedrooms with an indoor WC. Another document showed the plot had a large area of open space behind the building."

The first record of the house was in the 1878 Post Office Directory when Hill House was the only dwelling listed in Princes Road. It was occupied by Anne and John Cheal, a retired Fly Proprietor, and then in 1885 by a Mr George Collins who let out some of the land to a nurseryman. By 1889 it had changed hands again and was operating as a laundry, no doubt using the land as drying grounds. The business must have prospered as two extensions were built, the second of which was, in effect, the building which is now number 48, a purpose-built laundry. By 1890 Hill House was one of nine laundries in Princes Road (see chapter on Laundries).

By 1957 both nos 48 and 50 had been bought by Mr Fisher, who owned the Golf Ball factory in Richmond Road (seepage 45). He lived in no. 50 but let out no. 48 to a succession of small businesses. It was at one time a tie factory, but in the 1960s was converted back to a house. Fisher wanted to site a factory on the land at the rear but planning permission was refused, so instead he erected 28 lock-up garages. In 1985 Hill House was sold by him and permission was granted to demolish the garages at the rear and build houses in their place.

The Sylvan Hill Lodge, c1907, the gardener's cottage, at the entrance to the extensive grounds. Note the high wall to the left of the picture that once surrounded the site

The grandest and most ostentatious part of Roundhill consisted of the four large, detached mansions of the Sylvan Hall Estate, the first three of which were built by the Colbatch family, They were Rose Hill Villa, Rosehill Cottage, Sylvan Lodge and Wakefield Villa and had three gatekeepers' cottages to ensure privacy. They were classic Victorian buildings. The gardens were landscaped to run into one another. Rose Hill Villa was the first to be built, around 1838. The Rosehill Cottage name gives a false impression of its size. Two large iron gates opened on to a long, tree-lined drive, and it was almost impossible to see the house from Ditchling Road. The other houses were built soon afterwards.

Rose Hill Villa, later known as Hill Lodge c1840 - 1951

Three of these grand houses became Halls of Residence for the Diocesan Training College across the road and changed their names to Halls, whilst Rose Hill Villa became Hill Lodge. In 1903 it suffered the indignity of having its large rooms divided by temporary partitions for the student teachers. Rosehill Cottage always remained a family house.

"I worked at Hill Lodge for three years up to 1939. My job was to assist the housekeeper with the cleaning. I shared a two bedroomed flat at the top of the house. I wore a maid's uniform and earned 30 shillings per month plus our food. Thirty girls and one housemistress lived at Hill Lodge. As we were staff we had to enter the house from the side, but I know the front door opened to show a large staircase. We had August, ten days at Christmas and Easter as holidays, but we only got half pay. I left when war was declared and the house was requisitioned by the Ministry of Defence in 1939."
Gladys Prevett

18

Sylvan Hall was the next to go and in 1920 it too was filled with student teachers. Wakefield Villa hung on until 1931, when it's 'four bedrooms, two reception rooms and usual domestic offices, with a side entrance and garden' became 'The Rookery' to the students. Rosehill Cottage, on the other hand, survived as a home for the Clarke family until 1939.

> '[My mother] did a couple of hours cleaning now and again for an old lady, Mrs Smith. She lived in a large house that stood in its own grounds in Wakefield Road. Sometimes my brother and I went down to see her after school and Mrs Smith would give us some fruit, or a pudding left over from her dinner.'
> **Olive Masterson in her book.**

In 1908, Mr F W Waller, since 1900 the head gardener of Sylvan Lodge, gave an interview to 'Garden Life' describing the gardens.

> 'They [the gardens] are remarkable not only for natural beauty, but also because they show how much may be achieved by good judgement and skillful gardening in practically the heart of Brighton.'
> **F W Waller**

He described it as an all-the-year-round garden with thousands of bulbs in the spring, shrubs and trees along the carriageway, arriving at a house covered with clematis and passion-flowers. The grounds of the house included a bowling green, ornamental pond, tennis courts, kitchen garden and pleasure grounds.

In 1945 the Colbatch-Clark family put forward a plan for the whole estate to be developed as private apartments. Brighton Council was seriously short of land to provide new houses and under new compulsory purchase legislation it bought the estate and developed it for Council housing, broadly following the original private plans. The mansions were demolished: Rose Hill Villa (Hill Lodge), in 1948, Wakefield Lodge in 1951 and Sylvan Hall in the mid 1970s. Before the old houses disappeared one person explored them.

"I went into the old house [The Cottage] at the corner of Ditchling Road and Upper Lewes Road when it was derelict. I went upstairs, as I walked across the floor it gave way. I fell down onto the floor below and my foot went into a nail on the floorboard. My mate had to stand on the board to keep it still whilst I pulled my foot out."
Peter Foreman

Sylvan Hall was an annex to the Diocesan Training College for Schoolmistresses from 1920-1939. Students are sitting at a table on the left

Though they were Council owned the flats they were built to a high standard, with two or three bedrooms and two balconies. There were resident caretakers and gardeners. Qualification for residency was a strict means test, with tenants having to have an income above a certain level, but below a level whereby home ownership was a possibility. No young children below school age were permitted.

"I lived in The Lindens from 1952. I may be mistaken, but I think you had to earn about £500 a year, because the rents were higher. There were teachers, nurses and engineers in the flats. We stayed there for five years and then moved to another block The Poplars. The great thing was the wonderful grounds that the children could play in, in perfect safety, the best place to grow up in Brighton, with a good sense of community. A rent increase was threatened and we formed an association. I was sorry to leave in lots of ways."
Connie French

The Godly Gothic Building

The large knapped flint building, standing at the junction of Viaduct and Ditchling Roads, stands out amidst the much smaller scale houses surrounding it. It started life as Rosehill College and later became the Diocesan Training College, built in 1854 to a design by W & E Habershon on land bought from the Stanford family. Scott & Cawthorne extended the college in 1886. When, in 1887, an application to widen Ditchling Road was made the original walls of the college on the east side were knocked down and rebuilt with new entrance gates.

The College was one of two set up in the Diocese by an organisation called the National Society for the Education of the Poor in the Principles of the Established Church which was formed in 1811 and took over most of the schools already established by the Society for the Propagation of Christian Knowledge. By 1851 it controlled over 17,000 schools but the 1870 Education Act setting up the Board Schools, led to its decline. However the training of women teachers for the National Society schools in Sussex was carried out at Rose Hill up until the Second World War. The college included a 'Model and Practising School' to enable the schoolmistresses to have experience of teaching children. Local children who showed academic potential were selected to attend this school for extra tuition.

"My stepmother was proud that she had been one of two pupils selected from Preston National School to attend the 'Model School' for extra teaching. She attended one day a week and returned to Preston School for the other four days. She wanted to stay on at school and train as a teacher, but at that time [1901], her family needed her to go out to work at the age of thirteen to help with the family finances. She did a series of unskilled jobs until her marriage. She remembered her time at the school and encouraged me to do well academically. I later became a teacher myself.' E. A.

The young women who attended the college were carefully selected and did not come from the poorest homes. In 1875 the college prospectus stated that the college was for:

> 'Young women of eighteen years and upwards, duly recommended, and passed by the Government Examiners at the Entrance Examination in December annually, are received into residence for a fixed period of two years, to be trained as Mistresses of National Schools. Admission Fee £6, which includes all expenses (except for books and stationery) during the two years residence.'

Royal Engineers, Records & Pay Dept, Brighton. 1290.

22

Originally the students slept in the college building, with curtains surrounding each bed. They were well chaperoned by their tutors who accompanied them to church and to social events outside the college. From 1910 the students had their sleeping accommodation in Hill Lodge and later also in Sylvan Hall, on the other side of Ditchling Road.

The Training College continued to thrive until 1939, when a reorganisation of the Diocesan Training Schools was required because of the fall in the national birth rate. Instead of seizing the opportunity to lower the class numbers in the overcrowded elementary schools, the government decided that fewer elementary schoolmistresses would be required and funding was withdrawn from the Diocesan Council. Unfortunately Brighton was one of three colleges selected for closure and the premises were put up for auction in 1939. The Salvation Army was interested in purchasing the building for use as a hostel but before this scheme was able to progress the government requisitioned the site for the Royal Engineers' Records Office. From 1939 until 1987 the Ministry of Defence continued to use the building as offices.

"A recruitment drive took place at the Royal Engineers Records Office. I took the aptitude test in 1939 and started work the same day aged 17. It was an imposing building known as 'The College' and I worked in the post room. There were several girls tracing letters and parcels that had been posted to soldiers who had been moved to other units."
Doreen Blake

During the 1960s a modern extension was built at the back of the building, but in the 1980s the site was declared surplus to requirements and planning permission was requested to demolish the buildings and build houses. Many people were outraged by the proposal. The Brighton Society wrote to the Department of the Environment urging that the building should be listed, but this was refused as the chimneys had been removed. That decision was later reversed and the building was listed grade II. It was then bought and converted for use as the 'Brighton Business Centre', officially opening in 1988.

Opposite: The Diocesan Training College, now the Brighton Business Centre

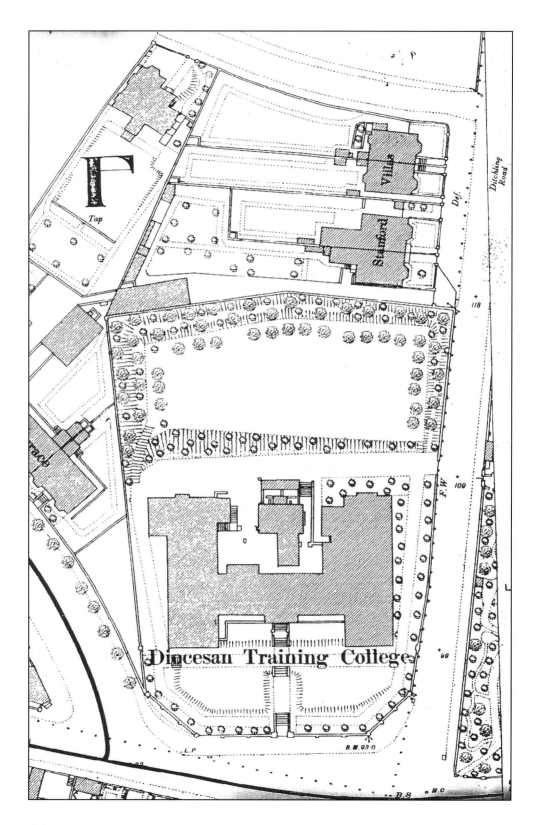

F

Tap

Diocesan Training College

Ditching Road

24

Three: Industries

Industry in Brighton has always meant service industry. The Roundhill area, more than most, demonstrates how much Brighton has always depended on small and often family-run concerns to provide employment. From nurseries and smallholdings through to laundries, a dustyard, and an abbatoir, as well as a well known pill factory, what was once a hive of local business activity has now become largely residential.

In the change from working locality to living locality is the whole story of the shifting pebbles and progress of Brighton's changing employment patterns. It all started with a windmill that had more names attached to it over time than there were uses for the grain it ground.

Tower Mill

Probably the most well known feature of the Roundhill area is the windmill that used to stand on the summit of the hill, at the north end of Belton Road,. The mill dated from 1838 and survived until 1913, a landmark for miles around. It was known at various times as: Rose Hill Mill, Round Hill Mill, Cutress's Mill, but normally Tower Mill. It is depicted on the sign of the Round Hill public house and on the end wall of several Forfars baker's shops. It appears on paintings and prints, and an early photograph shows the mill within a large fenced off area, with a shop on the left belonging to Mr Cutress, corn and seed chandler.

> 'The mill was an imposing building: 'Sixty feet high, with a copper domed top, and sails more than thirty-two feet long; the walls of the base were over two feet thick. There was also a wide base for the storage of sacks of corn. Fifty thousand bricks were used in its construction and the revolving top ran on a walnut stage.'
> **H T Dawes**

The mill stood 223 feet above sea level, and in 1838 would have looked over a rural landscape. The millers suffered mixed fortunes. In 1851 William Ford owned the mill, but was in financial difficulties by 1858. By 1862 the mill was closed awaiting a buyer; and it was not until 1868 that Thomas Turner Brazier took it over. By 1874/5 the fortune of the mill was still in

Opposite: map of the garden of the Diocesan Training College in 1877

decline since in that year its rateable value was dropping. In 1880 Charles Cutress, the founder of Forfars bakery, had bought it. He installed a steam engine to work the wheels and had the sails fastened, though this did not prevent the mill losing a sail in a storm.

Roundhill Road c1905 showing Cutress Mill and shop. The mill was demolished in 1913

In 1913, by now surrounded by houses, the mill was no longer required and was demolished, the bricks being cleaned and used to build the houses at the upper end of Belton Road. There are workshops and garages at the top of Roundhill Street overlooking the site of the windmill, and Cutress's bakery shop at the top left of Roundhill Road is now used as a workshop.

"I don't know when the Cutress family built the houses in Belton Road but we rented our house, no 24 [from them] at first; then we had a notice that Kate Cutress was wanting to sell some of the houses … and ours was one of them."
Mrs. Clarke

Nurseries and Smallholdings

Alongside the Mill a series of smallholdings and nurseries began to develop along the lower southern, sunny slopes as early as 1838. Rosehill Nursery, situated on Rose Hill East, was owned by Messrs J & G Evans, and was recorded as being:

> 'cultivated with great spirit - with crops of grapes, a splendid show of geraniums and other greenhouse plants, and the whole garden in the very highest order and keeping.'

One of the vineries was 45 ft in length and 10 ft in breadth and the weight of grapes cut annually from this vinery was three and a half cwt. In the same year there is the first mention of 'Verbena Nursery' in Upper Lewes Road owned by Mr Ansell.

> **The Brighton Herald of 13 January 1855** advertised a public auction of crops from the Conservative Land Society: 'The crops of fifteen acres (planted upon the above estate), consisting of wheat, rye, tares, strawberries, spinach, cabbage, onions, and other dinner requisites; also, many of the choicest specimens of Flora's kingdom.'

> **In May 1858 'The Brighton Herald'** advertised: 'Fuchsia Cottage Nursery in Park Crescent Road with three hot houses and ground, at £30 per year, stock by valuation. Choice and select variety of greenhouse plants just coming into bloom'

The nurseries flourished through the middle of the century but were gradually sold for building from the 1880s. The Salvation Army Citadel was built on the site of Rosehill Nursery in 1883, but Fuchsia Cottage continued to function as a market garden until the 1890s. Verbena Nursery continued to trade until even 1937 when the site became derelict. In 1985 the house at Verbena Nursery had been unlived in for many years and there were complaints from local residents who thought that the site was an eyesore. The owner of the house, Mr Gordon Camping, submitted plans for permission to build a three-storey block of 17 flats, and inevitably the once flourishing garden centre was demolished.

"I remember the nursery in Upper Lewes Road in the 1930s. It always looked run down and didn't seem to do much trade.'
Eileen Gower

Other small nurseries existed in the area. In Princes Road in 1875 there was a nursery overlooking the railway line and later another behind nos. 48 & 50. In the 1920s and 30s a smallholding called 'Crescent Nursery' was run by the McCullum family on land in Belton Road which abutted 1-11 Princes Terrace. Garages were built on the land in the 1950s and in 2004 houses were constructed and the area called Roundhill Mews.

Roundhill has an orchard that still survives. It is divided by the Roundhill Cat Creep between Wakefield Road and Roundhill Crescent; a locked door from the cat creep leads into it. It is probably the remains of the Verbena Nursery that once stood below the site.

Verbena Nursery in 1905: it opened in Upper Lewes Road in the 1860s. The glass houses are in front of the rear of Wakefield Road. The house was demolished in the 1980s

"The orchard lay behind the greenhouse wall of 14 Wakefield Road, a real treasure trove of apples, pears and cherries. The ground of the orchard sloped away from number 14 down towards the houses of Upper Lewes Road and most of the 'good' fruit was on the trees nearest to those houses. It wasn't long (before) I began my excursions into the orchard, returning with pockets bulging with fruit."
Colin Mather

28

Adjacent to this L shaped orchard stretches a wildlife paradise. Several of the houses in Richmond Road have extra gardens, created from the former land that lay between the original back gardens. One of these gardens, owned by Jan & Rusty Curry, won The Daily Telegraph/Wildlife Trust's Wildlife Garden of the Year competition in 2002. Even chicken and ducks were a common feature in the Roundhill area:

"…There was a gap between the houses of 30 and 36 (Roundhill Crescent) where there was a fence made out of old railway sleepers …behind that were the drying grounds for the old Northern Laundry which was in Upper Lewes Road. …There was a spare piece of ground which we rented - and kept chicken and ducks down there - that went from the back of 36 right along to 58 where there was a narrow gap between the houses."
Winifred Patchin

Allotments bordered the railway embankment. Local people would pick strawberries along – technically - railway property *"although railway bosses received strawberries for jam-making so they never complained about the practice."*

Sadly today's demands for housing have threatened many of the remaining small pockets of green in the area that are still a joy to local residents and home to wild life.

Map: 1875 showing nurseries and glass houses north of Park Crescent

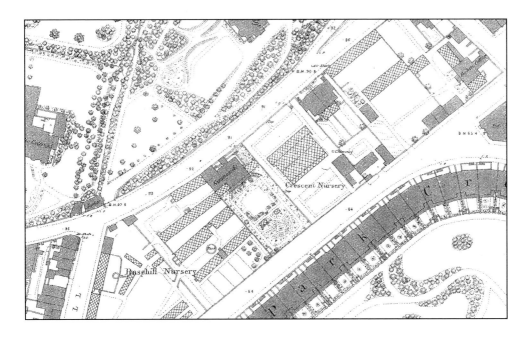

30

The Parish Dustyard

The 1810 Brighton Town Act enabled appointed 'scavengers' to collect the town's domestic rubbish and night soil. The Brighton Parish dustyard opened on the northern side of Dog Kennel Road (the present Upper Hollingdean Road), to enable the rubbish to be sorted and disposed of. In May 1866 a 'dust destructor' was established on this site to enable incineration to take place. The clinker that remained was then used as material for the construction of pavements, roads and playing fields.

A high wall surrounded the dustyard. The works consisted of a wharf with a yard for the deposit and sorting of the refuse. Later a railway ran by the side of the wharf for a proportion of the refuse to be taken away. Eventually there was 'a twelve-cell destructor, with four cremators, and two dust screens', along with a tall chimney and a yard where the clinker was deposited prior to its removal.

The building of the incinerator with its huge chimney in 1898 created a flurry of complaints. The Council minutes of 18 August 1899 showed a letter of complaint from Mr J. L. Thompson alleging a smell from the Refuse Destructor and asked if the Committee intended to do anything about the matter. A letter from the Reverend W. W. Palmer also complained of unpleasant smells from the chimney and the matter was referred to the Council's Surveyor. At the same meeting an offer was made by Mr A. J. Evans to purchase all the waste iron at the destructor for six pence per ton.

However, in the Council minutes of July 1900, a letter from Messrs Davey Bros still complained of the smell and they were informed that the smell did not come from the destructor but from the heap of clinkers that had become fired and fused.

Considerable resistance to the development of the dust destructor continued in the area. Owners of small laundries in the Roundhill and Hollingdean areas complained of 'dirty debris' or 'blacks' [smuts] floating onto their laundry. There was also criticism of the Corporation for depositing refuse from carts on land in Roedale Road and bricks and refuse in the roadway.

Dust Destructor at Hollingdean c1902: looking across what was then called the Ash Yard and Corporation Stone Works to the Hollingdean allotments, showing the laying of railway lines to connect with the Brighton to Lewes line. To the left is the entrance to Roedale Road and the Hollingbury Hotel.

A Surveyor, Mr Tulloch, was appointed to investigate the complaints and he visited destructors at Cambridge, Leicester and Shoreditch in order to compare facilities. His report, presented to the Council in 1898, stated that:

> 'There is no Dust destructor, nor indeed any chimney in the world, the fumes from which are always invisible or even harmless and from which a discharge of harmless matter is not always taking place and can be prevented from doing so. ... We do not want to commit the ratepayers to the very large additional expenditure and waste of money which doing away with the works would involve. I have repeatedly stood in the very midst of the refuse while all the operations of tipping it from the carts onto the yard and of sorting and sifting the materials have been carried on. I have not experienced anything but a faint odour that has been imperceptible when I have walked away a few paces off. When I left the yard and walked in the roads and streets close by I have never been able to detect the slightest nuisance, nor have I observed any flies that are always a sure indication of the presence of offending matters'.

There were plans to use the heat from the chimney to generate steam for the machines of neighbouring factories, but it is doubtful whether this was ever put into practice.

In spite of the original complaints, the Dust Destructor remained until 1952 when incineration ceased and household rubbish was taken to Sheepcote Valley. The Hollingdean Destructor then became redundant and the chimney, by now a familiar landmark in Brighton, was demolished in 1962. Two large blocks, called Nettleton Court & Dudeney Lodge, each containing 87 flats, were built c1966 near the site, which now dominate the skyline even more than the old chimney.

Today the area is still used by the Environmental Services as a depot for street cleaners and rubbish lorries, and there is renewed controversy about where to build a new incinerator to deal with rubbish from the City of Brighton & Hove.

The Abattoir

The Municipal Abattoir was built in 1894 so that the many highly unsanitary slaughterhouses in the poorer areas of the town could be removed. The nearest abattoirs to Roundhill at that time would have been in Oxford Court (see 'Backyard Brighton') and Providence Place. The Hollingdean site was not the first chosen by the Council for an abattoir, as land in the Prestonville area (Stanford Road) had already been designated. The Hollingdean site was undoubtedly further away from the expensive houses of Dyke Road, and, being close to the Dust Destructor, it kept the council's utility services together. The abattoir was served by a small siding branching off the main Brighton to Lewes railway, with the junction just north of the Kemp Town line. The siding could not be accessed directly from the Brighton Goods Yard, trains being required to proceed as if going to Lewes, then reverse back into the siding from just beyond the Hollingdean Bridge. Later, the council used adjacent spare land for the wholesale meat market, and the town's Cleansing Station where infested belongings and people were deloused.

Houses within the privately enclosed depot and abbatoir are approached by a narrow road leading from 154 Ditchling Road, just opposite the Skew Bridge, taken before 1962. Note the octagonal building in the Jewish cemetery to the left and the chimney of the Dust Destructor on the right

Simeon Elliot had vivid memories of the abattoir, as his grandfather was a wholesale butcher based near the main slaughterhouse. His grandfather, Mr Goldsmith, used to collect the carcasses directly from the slaughterman, cut them up into joints and these would be taken on a fleet of five lorries to the retail outlets. Life at the abattoir started early with the workers on site no later than six am, and the whole process was over by one pm.

"A colleague of my grandfather was Rabbi Joseph, who came to wash and bless the meat to ensure that it was kosher. He had a little office to the left of the abattoir gates. My grandfather was always telling stories of escaped cattle, but I never saw any myself."

The job was not well paid but Simeon's grandfather was proud of his occupation. The family business closed when the abattoir itself was in decline. Local people remember the abattoir with mixed feelings:

"You could hear the mooing of the cattle going to slaughter,"
Ernest Austen

"The abattoir used to smell a bit. I used to go down the abattoir road to go to Lewes Road to get my bus. I used to smell it as I walked past."
Harold Ansell

"I was at Downs First School in about 1975. I remember the smell when I went out to play. It was really overpowering, a sort of metallic and yet fetid smell. I've never smelled anything like it since. It was amazing that no one thought of this when they located the new building. If you asked anyone what it was, they said, 'the abattoir', but nobody was very forthcoming."
Allie Rogers

The abattoir failed to meet modern hygiene standards, even after the council leased it to private enterprise, and it closed in 1986. Some meat traders are still located there, and the Cleansing Station also remains, though boarded up as it is seldom used nowadays.

Laundries

'you arrive at the unprotected summit of the hills, open to every breath of heaven, and principally tenanted by washerwomen'

W. Kebbell writing in 1848

Small laundries developed in Roundhill, as the opportunity to have drying grounds high above the smoky town enabled them to develop in individual houses, which later grew into larger businesses.

Street directory advertisement for the Brighton and Sussex Laundry Works 1888

By 1875 there were already a number of laundries listed in Lewes and Upper Lewes Roads, mostly small concerns. Upper Lewes Road however contained the large Brighton & Sussex Laundry Works (on the site of the present Sainsburys) which provided employment for many women in the area. In the 1880s the Brighton & Sussex Laundry was advertising 'Washing, Clear Starching, Glazing, Calendering, Scouring and Hot Pressing with no washing powders or preparations of any description used on the premises'. Special arrangements could be made with schools, lodging houses and hotels, and a van called daily to all parts of the town. A large open drying ground was advertised as being attached. The Brighton & Hove

Laundry moved to larger premises in Hove in 1910 and Cox's Pill Factory took over the site.

"My mother's family lived in Newmarket Street at the turn of the century. My maternal grandmother, Mrs Ticehurst, my mother and all my aunts worked at the Brighton & Sussex Laundry at the end of Upper Lewes Road. My mother only worked there before her marriage but she considered it a good job, especially as it was so near her home. The laundry specialised in 'fast call in' which meant that they did very quick work and they were the 'cat's whiskers' at their job. They were lucky to have Lewes Road station just behind them that allowed giant hampers of washing to arrive from the big country houses in Sussex. I think my mother really enjoyed her time at the laundry, although it was often very hot, hard work. She used to speak of the good times she had with the other laundry girls when they had finished work and went for a 'knees up' in the Gladstone Pub in Lewes Road."
Harry Bull

Women working in the Mayo Laundry in Mayo and Richmond Roads c1910

By 1881 more residential streets had been developed in the Roundhill area and many home laundries were being set up, mainly in the Princes and Richmond Road area. These houses had gardens that were ideal as drying grounds and some enterprising families bought top sections of the adjacent gardens to extend their drying areas. Some of these T shaped gardens still exist today. Princes Road had laundries at numbers 39, 48, 50, 53, 57 & 60.

A blight on the local laundry industry at this time was the construction of the dust destructor in Hollingdean Road. Complaints were made to the Council about the smoke and 'blacks' that were coming from the large chimney (see The Parish Dustyard page 31).

Some family laundries, such as the Winter family laundry in Mayo Road, developed into larger concerns:

"My grandfather, who was born in Poynings, came to live in Brighton at 29 Richmond Road and worked as a gardener. The family moved to a small house at 6 Mayo Road where my grandmother started to take in washing. She became so successful that she told my grandfather to stop the gardening and come to help her in the laundry. He bought a horse and cart for collecting and delivering the laundry and it started a family business that ran for over 100 years.

They had eight children, six daughters and two sons. The daughters all worked in the laundry that my grandmother ran until she was 84. She always worked until one week before the birth of each child and then employed a nanny, so that she could return to work. After her death her two sons Harry and Frederick carried on the business. Grandmother always insisted that the girls who worked for her were properly dressed, with no curlers in their hair and no scarves on their heads. Most of the workers were local women, and three sisters actually worked for the laundry for 50 years. Even after they retired they used to come into the laundry and help for a couple of hours a day. We had a loyal staff, but we would often compete with Cox's Pill Factory in Lewes Road for the same girls.

The business was gradually built up. In the 1920s there were 90 women working there and the premises were extended. Men were employed to collect and deliver the laundry and maintain the equipment, but the majority of workers were women, who were strictly supervised by my grandmother. The jobs were divided into those who sorted and packed, washers who had the hardest job in the heat and steam, ironers, and the workers on the calenders where sheets were fed through a large roller. You had to be quick at this job or you could get your fingers caught. The packers were top of the hierarchy, as the work was clean and dry,

The Mayo Laundry c1910

Ironing was originally done by hand with coke stoves to heat the irons. Later there were gas irons with the gas piped from overhead. It would take two people to iron a large tablecloth; a goffering machine would be used for collars.

The girls worked long hours during the week and on Saturday morning. If there was a rushed job they would work extra hours and share the work with other laundries in the area. The customers were originally from the large houses. We would have customers from Palmeira Square and the large hotels. We even went to Birchgrove for Harold Macmillan's laundry.

We became a limited company in 1918. The account books have been kept since that date. Before that date the vans were horse drawn, but some of the horses had been requisitioned for war work in World War One and so a motor van was bought. During that war two of my aunts drove the van. When mechanisation started coming in my grandmother borrowed £10 to buy the first washing machine, and didn't sleep properly until she had paid it back. In 1945 we still had 45 workers but by the time we closed we only had 20.

It wasn't the launderettes that made us decide to close but increasing costs, and finally losing business to 'Linen Hire'. Most customers were very loyal but increasingly large companies took over the hotels, and they didn't want to be involved with the laundry and employed firms to arrive each week with clean linen and take the dirty linen away.

The company closed in 1984 and the land was sold for building. Mayo Court now stands on the site."
Donald Winter

"After the Second World War [there were] extensions to the boiler room [at the Mayo laundry] and number 31 Richmond Road was demolished."
Ron Burleton

"Our grandparents, Frederick & Ellen Bowden, took over the laundry at 28 Crescent Road in 1898 and lived in the house next door. The vans would collect the washing in wicker baskets and take it straight to the sorting room. If there wasn't a laundry mark it would be marked with coloured cotton. The clothes were then put into separate bins, taken to the washhouse - steamy and noisy, with belts chugging all the time. Our father supervised the washhouse where only men worked, as it was heavy work. The washing was put to dry and then taken up the rickety stairs to the ironing room. The room contained a coal fire with ledges all round where the big, heavy irons stood. The women took the irons and rushed back to the benches to iron the clothes. When the irons cooled they rushed back to replace the cooling iron and take another hot iron in its place. Towels were not ironed and not put through the calender because it would make them go hard but they were pegged up on a wire in the garden to dry. A couple of girls did the shirt and collar dressing. Downstairs was the calender room. The calender had two big rollers and two girls would feed the sheets through the rollers and they would then be folded by the girls the other side. The machine was very hot to touch and if the sheets were slightly out they would have to do it all again.
In the packing room the girls sorted out the laundry by using the laundry book for each customer. The laundry would be wrapped in a piece of tissue paper and put into hampers ready for the van run. The girls worked very long hours, 8am - 7pm on some occasions and also on Saturdays. They all wore wrapover overalls with nothing on their heads. When it was time to go home a piece of string would be pulled and a hooter would sound. The girls dressed quickly and all ran down the local streets to their homes. The laundry did a lot of regular hotel work that kept the laundry busy at all times.
The Primrose Laundry was also in Crescent Road and we often did some of their laundry because we were bigger. We could get to their laundry by a back way behind the houses. At the back of the laundry there was a drying

ground that backed onto Belton Road. My father had a rifle range in that area.

Grandma died first and father took over the laundry while granddad was still alive. Father eventually sold the laundry, but didn't make much profit, as times were changing and the 1960s had seen the growth of launderettes and later people had their own washing machines."

Barbara Petrarca & Brenda Ashong

Other laundries were founded including the Tivoli and Primrose Laundries in Crescent Road

"I was born in Sun Street in Brighton in 1889. I went to work in a laundry when I was 14 in 1903. My sister worked for the hand laundry in Crescent Road. The sheets and tablecloths were sent to the steam laundry and those big calenders, but we did all the small stuff. There were two big coppers in the corner and you used to have to poke them down.

Mr Bowden used to take two ponies and a trap to collect the washing. Everything was white in those days and it was washed and ironed by hand, even the lace curtains. Although it was hard work I was happy, I was with the firm until I was 85. I'd stand at that machine and I'd sing songs and the ironers used to sing with me. "

Jessie Robinson

"Emily Laycock, my great-grandmother, took in laundry and from the 1890s the family lived at 43 & 44 Upper Lewes Road, with extensive drying

grounds at the back that stretched to Roundhill Crescent. The family continued running the laundry that became known as 'The Northern Laundry' until the 1960s. I remember going to visit my grandparents there in the 1950s and 60s. Even as a child I was struck at how primitive it all was. There appeared to be very little mechanisation and I think they had a hard life. My grandmother had a squashed thumb where she had caught it in a mangle; my grandfather limped from an accident in the laundry. Every evening my grandfather would go out in his van to collect the roller towels from the corporation premises and replace them with fresh ones, as they had the laundry contract for the Council. They retired in the 1960s and sold the premises and the land behind that I believe was used to build some modern houses fronting Roundhill Crescent. They didn't appear to make much money from the sale though, as they both went to work for a laundry in Hove."

Ann Nealer

"There was grass over the drying field that ran from Roundhill Crescent down to Upper Lewes Road market … and always seemed to have towels or nappies in it, it seemed be full of white squares … never a variety of laundry."

Winifred Patchin

Mrs. Poole's family used to run the Aberdeen Laundry at 23 Upper Lewes Road.

"When I was a child they had a laundry receiving office. People used to take their washing there and they would send it on to a laundry and people came to collect it from there later. As a child I used to deliver some of the parcels to about four people who were special customers. … Men wore separate stiff white collars to shirts, so they sent them to be laundered. They used to be like boards, really hard, horrible!"

Mrs. Joyce Poole

Home laundries still existed in the area alongside the larger companies. These would deal with the small personal laundry rather than regular work from hotels and large houses. In 1905 Mrs Neale of 53 Princes Road advertised her laundry services in the local directory as

> 'All work being done by hand there is no risk as in steam power. Large open drying grounds – moderate terms.'

"The little laundries used to do a 'bag wash'. You had an empty bag and you filled it with as much as you could get in for three pence. You put it on your doorstep and they came and collected it, washed it, partly dried it and brought it back in the sack."
Mrs. Gausden

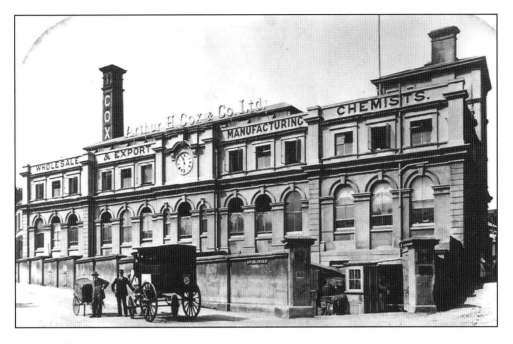

Cox's Pill Factory c1914. Erected in the 1860s as the Brighton and Hove Steam Laundry (see page 35), now the site of Sainsburys supermarket

By 1900 the laundries were the largest employers in the area. Gradually they disappeared, firstly the home laundries in the 1930s and then all the large laundries by the 1980s. The advent of the launderette and the home washing machine both contributed to the decline of Roundhill's largest industry. The only reminder of those times when Roundhill could be called 'Laundry Hill' are the faded signs, as in Crescent Road, and hidden T shaped drying grounds in the back gardens of the houses on the hill.

Cox's Pill Factory

In 1871 Arthur Hawker Cox split his business, which started in Ship Street in 1839, into two parts. He handed the shop in Ship Street to his son Homersham Edward but he retained the manufacturing part of the business for himself and moved to new premises at 10a St Martin's Place.

Arthur Cox had experimented in coating pills with a tasteless non-metallic film with 'an elegant pearl like appearance'. So effective was the coating in completely disguising the various unpleasant tastes that he was able to claim that pills

> 'may be kept in the mouth for several minutes without taste,
> though soluble in a short time even in cold water'.

In 1854 he had applied for, and was granted, a patent for this discovery. The first price list issued from St Martin's Place shows a range of 331 products being manufactured. Hospitals and other public institutions were supplied at special rates and all pills were sent free, on the same day as the order was received. Cox's patent for tasteless coating had expired in 1870, but in order to encourage the customers to remain loyal the catalogue repeatedly warned 'Beware of Imitations'.

Arthur Hawker Cox died in 1903. The Brighton Herald printed an obituary of 'one of Brighton's most venerable and most noted citizens'. The children of Arthur Cox were left shares in the company but two sons, Arthur Hawker Cox ll and Edward Edwards Cox held the majority.

In February 1910 negotiations were begun with the owners of the Brighton and Sussex Laundry in Lewes Road, initially for a yearly tenancy of the premises, but it was then decided that the premises should be purchased at a price of £5,500. The directors discussed the question of a 'turret timepiece' at the new factory. Messrs Lawson, Pearce, Barfott & Loudon were given the order at £45 (the price was reduced by £5 for permission to put their own name on the clock). In 1912 the company began the process of building and adapting the laundry premises into the factory that was to continue for the next 60 years.

Some employees joined the armed forces during the early stages of the First World War, and after conscription in 1916 the company found it difficult to obtain men, materials or finance. There were also difficulties with transport as the Government controlled the railways. and freight was expensive and scarce. Although they obtained Government contracts the cost of materials outweighed the advantages, as Government contracts were not so profitable. For almost two years after the Armistice, industrialists enjoyed a post war boom, but when the bubble burst in October 1920 and Cox, like many others, found that orders stopped abruptly.

The Cox's were benevolent employers, up to a hundred employees were taken on annual outings, one for men and one for women. Several generations of the same families came to work at Cox's.

In 1939 A H Cox & Co celebrated its centenary, but at the start of the Second World War they again lost half their staff to active service. The burden of running the business fell on Edward Cox, now in his sixties, and his sister-in-law Lettice Mackie. More women were recruited at Cox's and Rose Lee, a former bus conductress, supervised them. Much production during the war was for Government contracts, though at the same time the company tried to maintain its service to its regular customers.

Edward Cox died in 1950. He was an austere and gentlemanly figure who struck fear into some of his junior employees with his twice-daily tour of the factory. The company continued to thrive throughout the 50s and 60s but it became apparent that modernisation and expansion were necessary if they were to continue to manufacture in Brighton. In spite of attempts by the company to relocate within the Brighton area, in 1979 the company moved to Barnstable, ending sixty-nine years of manufacturing the sugar coated pills in Upper Lewes Road.

"I worked at Cox's Pill Factory from 1952 to 1955. There were about twenty other girls who all started on the same day, most of them were from Moulsecoomb or Whitehawk. We used to listen to the radio and sing songs while we worked. In the evening we would go dancing or to the cinema. I worked from 8.00 am until 5.30 pm, Monday to Friday and sometimes did overtime on Saturday mornings. I did a bit of everything, filling the pill bottles, making up orders, labelling. The pills were made in the pill department and then sent through to the bottle department. We labelled the bottles and put the pills into machines on the conveyor belt. When I first started work I earned 36 shillings per week but after one month I got two pounds per week and five shillings for Saturday morning overtime."
Valerie Slade

Fisher's Golf Ball Factory

William Fisher set up a golf ball recycling factory at 21-23 Richmond Road in the 1920s. He purchased the semi-detached villas from the Army and gutted the ground floors to create a factory, using the upper floors for raw materials and storage. He installed a coke boiler in the basement to generate electricity to power the machinery. Golf balls were recovered and re-sold under the brand names of Maxims or Saxon. By the 1930s, the factory was successful and Mr. Fisher employed some 30 people, a level of staffing which remained until 1945.

During the Second World War all the buildings were used for munitions work, but afterwards they reverted to their former use until the 1970s, when they were sold to Phillips, a manufacturer of rubber goods, in particular 'Stick On Soles'. By the 1980s all this had finished and the premises were converted to a carpentry workshop. The buildings were converted back to housing in 1982, to some 20 flats.

"I left school in 1936 and went to work at the golf ball factory at 23 Richmond Road in one of the old three storey villas. My job was to unwind the elastic from the old golf balls and then they had to be rewound with new 'string' and dipped in white plastic. I didn't stay there long because I only got 2/6d a week."
Gladys Prevett

"Opposite [my house] was a golf ball factory. I worked part time for about eighteen months (in the late 1950s I think). There were about seventeen of us making or reconstituting the golf balls, plus two or three girls in the office. There were a surprising number of processes involved with the production … but nothing appeared to be streamlined, Women busied themselves in a rabbit warren of different rooms, emerging now and then to lug a bucket or an unwieldy tray of golf balls from one place to another."
Jan Curry

Above: Roundhill 1870; far right middle: Diocesan Training College; top far right: Elm Grove and the Workhouse now Brighton General Hospital; Ditchling Road from the Diocesan College: first house: Rose Hill Villa later called Hill Lodge; semi-detached house: Rose Hill Park Estate; small house at the back: possibly a gardener's or groom's house, now Downsview; Tower windmill with Princes Villa to the left of the mill, now Roundhill Road; row of small houses: Ranalagh Terrace now listed as Ditchling Road. The gap is now Princes Road. Warleigh Lodge; small farm cottages and the Jolly Huntsman Inn, now the Jolly Brewer public house, in Ditchling Road

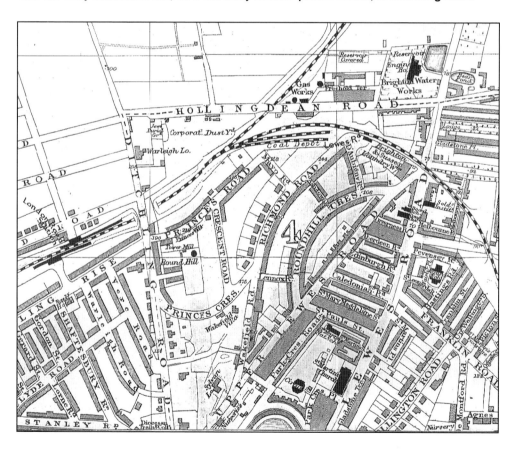

The Railway

The railways cut through the area and created a new artery. With increased possibilities for travel linked to work and leisure came the railway workers and their families. Rich and poor lived side by side in a more modern social mix. Roundhill was changing and re-casting itself. A residential area, more connected and less reliant on itself, was about to be born.

The Brighton to Lewes railway line opened in 1846, effectively dividing Roundhill into the southern and northern sections. A branch line to Kemp Town was opened in 1869, primarily to prevent the London, Chatham and Dover railway from building an alternative London to Brighton line via East Grinstead and Lewes with a terminus in Kemp Town. The impact of this branch line was not really noticeable in Roundhill until 1873, when Lewes Road station was opened. This station was reached by a brick path from D'Aubigny Road, and its opening gave the area direct access to Brighton main station and the huge railway locomotive and carriage works nearby. As a consequence railway workers started to move into the Roundhill area. In the 1881 census there are nine railway workers living in Wakefield Road with jobs ranging from stationmaster to porter. The incomplete Princes and Mayo Roads had nine and three resident railway workers respectively, whilst other railway workers lived in the surrounding streets.

"The manager of the Lancing carriage works lived at 37 Richmond Road and two engine drivers lived in Ashdown Road. A railway engineer and the signalman for Lewes Road station also lived in Richmond Road."
Ron Burleton

Whilst working for the Southern Railway, Ron Burleton travelled to his job daily from Lewes Road station, changing at Brighton for the express service to the Lancing works - the 'Lancing Belle' as it was commonly known.

"We used to live in that cottage at the bottom of Princes Road. It was a beautiful house and garden, with the signal box. We moved from the white cottage in 1989 after 29 years; the signal box should have gone to the Bluebell Railway but they didn't come to collect it, so it was demolished at the same time, 7am on Boxing Day 1989. It was my workshop. Anything we wanted to store we put in the signal box."
Ron French

Opposite: Ordnance Survey map of Brighton 1882 showing the railway lines

LEWES RD CONGREGATIONAL - CH. OUTING - 5/7/09.

48

Winifred Patchin remembered Lewes Road station as having an island platform and a main platform on the Richmond Road side linked by a footbridge. Winifred and Ron recalled the signalling technique in use at the time, that of a brass hand staff. This staff had to be handed over by the locomotive driver to the signalman as the train entered the single track to Kemp Town. It allowed the signalman to set the points and signals so that no other train could enter that line, and so avoiding a collision.

"We used to watch the driver hand over his metal rod. It was two feet long with brass bands around it, and he handed it over before he could go on the single track."
Winifred Patchin

There was a half hourly service from Lewes Road station, to both Kemp Town and Brighton:

"Very handy, quick too and cheap – I suppose a penny."
Mrs Clarke

Ernest Austen recalls the use of motor trains (similar to a rail-bus) rather than a train hauled by a locomotive. This change had occurred in 1905 when there was a need to economise on running costs, and when Hartington Road Halt had opened to try to boost the passenger numbers.

"The motor train would drop me off at Lewes Road station, and I would walk down D'Aubigny Road and Roundhill Crescent to my home in Upper Lewes Road. Working for the Gas Company at Lancing and Shoreham, I had a free three monthly season ticket to and from Brighton and that included the motor train to Kemp Town."
Ernest Austen

Apart from passenger traffic, Lewes Road station had a thriving coal yard, to service the Co-op. Winifred Patchin and her sisters recalled the early operation at the coal yard, when the coal trains would discharge their cargo into wooden chutes and thence into pens accessed by coal lorries and carts in Hollingdean Road. This would be roughly where Sainsburys currently stands. This was necessary since the other side of Lewes Road station, in Richmond Road, was for passenger traffic. When the passenger service ceased on 1 January 1933, the coal yard was gradually moved over to the Richmond Road side. The newsagent/tobacconist shop at the corner of

Opposite: Lewes Road Congregational Sunday school outing 1909 at Lewes Road station

Richmond Road and D'Aubigny Road became a Co-op fuel office and appeared to control the activity in the yard. The yard was to remain until the early 80s when it disappeared with the Sainsbury's development around 1984.

Lewes Road station was used for social activities, "We went to the Congregational church in Lewes Road and we used the Lewes Road station quite a lot for Sunday school treats. We hired a special train which took us into Brighton station and then to either Hassocks or Burgess Hill in alternate years, to the pleasure gardens there."
Winifred Patchin

"I can remember my brother going on the train from Lewes Road station for a Sunday school outing, but I wasn't old enough to go. So I went up to the station to see him off. He was only going to Littlehampton."
Mrs Joyce Poole

In 1933 the Lewes Road station was converted into the Victor Sauce and Pickle factory, but was derelict by 1952. The footbridge was removed and the buildings were gradually demolished to allow the builder's yard and the coal yard to expand. The line finally closed to freight in 1971 and the Lewes Road viaduct was demolished in 1976, though the stub end remained until 1983 when the Vogue Gyratory was developed.

View down New England Road c1870. On the right are the paired villas of Roundhill Park in Ditchling Road. The Tower windmill stands at the summit surrounded by fields. The road to the mill became Roundhill Road. Ranalagh Terrace runs to the north before the Roundhill Tavern was built. The roof of Princes Villa can be seen at the back

Four: Post Victorian Roundhill

The raunchy side of Roundhill, along with the sober growth of elementary education and schools used as hospitals in the First World War, all sound like the ingredients for a feature film. Proof that the area continued to sit centre stage in its own drama is the evidence provided in the story of its Post-Victorian era.

Raunchy Roundhill.

The staid Victorian mansion of Sylvan Hall figured on the fringe of a piece of rather colourful history later in its life, through the tenancy of the Meyrick family. In 1914 Dr Ferdinand Richard Holmes Meyrick took the lease of the Lodge with his wife Kate and eight children. Dr Meyrick had a good reputation for the care of the mentally ill and, with his wife's help, had run various nursing homes in Britain for them. They set up an establishment at Sylvan Hall, described by them as 'a lovely old world house at Brighton, where we were as secluded as though we had been in the depths of the country'. They obviously had wealthy, long-stay patients, but also took in badly shell-shocked soldiers. Dr. Meyrick was interested in hypnotism and alternative therapies and worked with chronic nerve cases. He had a surgery at 34 Wakefield Road.

Kate Meyrick assisted her husband and took on much of the responsibility for the patients' daily care. All through the First World War the Meyricks frequently provided entertainments in the grounds, sometimes to raise funds and sometimes for the soldiers.

In 1918 Kate Meyrick decided to leave her husband on account of his cruelty. She had eight children under the age of 21, the girls still attending Roedean School and the boys various public schools, and an allowance of 15 shillings per week to pay for it all. In order to support her family Kate Meyrick embarked on a life that was to bring her wealth and notoriety, linking her name with gambling and prostitution. She owned, or managed, half a dozen nightclubs during her career, but she remains linked in people's minds to the '43 Club' at 43 Gerrard Street in Soho. Her first club was opened in 1919 but within a few months the police raided it. In 1924 she was sentenced to six months imprisonment for selling alcohol outside permitted hours, after which she started to bribe the police.

She reached notoriety in January 1929 when she was tried at the Old Bailey in the 'Goddard Case', one of the most important police corruption trials of the century. She was convicted of bribing the police and sent to Holloway for 15 months. She served five jail sentences at various times totalling three years three months, but always returned to her night club career, entertaining leading personalities of the day from stage, screen, literature, the arts, politics, sport and even the King. She was universally known as Ma Meyrick and called the 'Queen of the London Clubs'.

Kate Meyrick died of broncho-pneumonia in January 1933 aged 57. She had seen her children prosper. All of them received a public school education and had been groomed for positions of social standing, three of her daughters marrying peers. Soon after the Meyricks left in 1923 Sylvan Hall welcomed the staid students from the Diocesan College.

Schools

In the mid 1800s Brighton was becoming known as 'school town', because of the many private day and boarding schools that were established in the area.

By 1875 there were several of these schools in Roundhill. At no 2 Roundhill Crescent Mrs Gravely taught music & singing, at no 31 Mrs Izard, wife of the manager of the Roundhill Estate office, ran private classes whilst Mrs Stephenson and Miss Walker opened a preparatory school for young gentlemen at number 50. Private schools continued to open in the Roundhill area until the 1920s.

The less affluent families who moved into the area after 1875 would have originally relied on charity and church schools to educate their children. St Martin's School opened in 1867, whilst Lewes Road Congregational Church Hall was used for lessons from 1878 until the opening of the Lewes Road Board School (later known as Fairlight) in 1892. The Roundhill area itself did not contain an elementary school for poorer parents who had to select one from the surrounding area for their children.

After the 1870 Education Act Board schools were built to provide elementary education up to the age of 12 or 13. The nearest Board Schools would have been Pelham Street, Hanover Terrace, Lewes Road and Ditchling Road. Hollingdean Road School opened at the foot of Hollingdean Road as a temporary prefabricated school in 1904 and closed in 1915. The opening of this temporary school indicates the high number of children coming into the area.

These 'temporary school' buildings then reopened as the 'Special School' for children who were recommended to attend by the Medical Officer, as they could not work alongside average children. The junior boys were taught the 3 R's plus rug making, raffia work, Indian basketry and drawing, whilst the older boys learnt carpentry and boot repairing. The junior girls hemmed garments to be sold and knitted socks and stockings, whilst the older girls made simple undergarments out of cotton and flannel, children's dresses and pinafores, and learnt housewifery and cookery. Others did basic clay work, bead threading, boot-lacing, and simple stitching with large needles and coloured wool. In the 1960s this prefabricated building was used by the local Technical College and was finally demolished in the late 1990s when the Latter Day Saints Church was built on the site.

In spite of the Board Schools' best efforts, local children had little opportunity of gaining much more more than a basic education. Boys were directed into manual work and girls to domestic employment after the age of 13. The local laundries and Cox's pill factory provided employment for many of the girls in the area.

St Martin's school in the background of St Martin's Street c1905. It has now been converted to flats

In 1907, a highly competitive, free-place system was introduced to enable children at the age of 11 to transfer from the elementary school to the secondary school. The number who were successful was small and did not satisfy demands for more children to receive secondary education. This examination provided a much needed scholarship system for working class children, but parents often found the cost of the uniform, or allowing an older child to continue with their education, a burden on household finances. Many children, particularly girls, were unable to accept their scholarship places.

Anne Hill's maternal family moved into 62 Richmond Road in 1906 and it remained the family home for forty years, sometimes with 12 people in the household. The family had moved from Gloucester Street in Brighton and the girls continued to attend Pelham Street School from their Richmond Road home.

"My grandfather, James Latham, was a journeyman tool maker, but with such a large family he wouldn't have been able to afford to send his daughters to secondary school if they hadn't passed the scholarship examination and obtained a 'Hedgecock Bequest'. Fortunately all three of his daughters passed the scholarship examination and were able to benefit from continuing their education."

Ditchling Road School had a very good reputation for pupils passing the scholarship examination and this made it a popular school. Other schools did have some successes as the records of Lewes Road Council School and St Martin's Church of England school show.

During World War One several of the schools were used as hospitals,

"I went to Pelham Street school. Of course that was the First World War … it was taken over by the hospital and some of us went to the upstairs of the Railway Mission in Viaduct Road, and some went opposite the Co-op until the war ended. Then we went back to Pelham Street … but I wasn't there long before I was 14 and I left school."
Mrs Clarke

Lewes Road and St Martin's Schools attracted the children who lived on the eastern side of Roundhill, whilst Pelham Street and Ditchling Road Schools attracted the children on the western side. Whichever school was selected, walking some distance to school seemed inevitable. Winifred Patchin remembered the journey to Varndean School in the 1930s. From her home in Roundhill Crescent, she had to walk either up the cat creep or via Ashdown Road and Richmond Road, to reach Princes Crescent and then the long ascent up Ditchling Road to Varndean.

"You could get a tram from St Saviour's to Fiveways, but it wasn't worth it because you still had to walk the rest of the way up to the school. Everyone walked, the schoolteachers, even the Headmistress; no one had cars."
Varndean Boys' School was built three years after the Girls' School and the distance travelled by some pupils to the two Varndeans meant that the schools provided school dinners.

Winifred Patchin recalls,*"We turned our noses up at school dinners, but otherwise you had to take sandwiches, … it was the first time we had been offered school dinners."*

Lewes Road School was temporarily closed during the World War Two, after the bombing of the Franklin Inn and houses in Caledonian Road on 20 September 1940, and pupils transferred to Elm Grove School. Mrs Poole was a pupil at Lewes Road School during this time:

"We did mornings one week and afternoons the next week because we had to share schools, … the schools had shelters outside in the road, oval shaped buildings where we sat if the air raid siren went off. We didn't mind it too much since it was an excuse to miss lessons. We didn't realise what the war was all about."

After the 1944 Education Act and the reorganisation of the schools, St Martin's, Lewes Road (now Fairlight), Ditchling Road (now Downs) and Pelham Street schools all became infant and junior schools. Pelham Street subsequently closed but St Martin's, Fairlight and the Downs continue to educate the children of Roundhill.

The Brighton and Hove Orphan Boys Home

In 1869 a large house called 'Bryn' was built on the corner of Wakefield and Upper Lewes Roads. The house is still noticeable because the garden wall juts out at an angle at the bottom of Wakefield Road creating difficulties for any traffic turning into Upper Lewes Road.

In 1875 the house became the 'Brighton Boys' Brigade Home'. It remained a Boys' Home for 62 years. By the 1880s it was called the 'Brighton Free Home for Destitute and Orphan Boys', who advertised that their policy was 'to shelter, feed and clothe destitute orphan boys, between the ages of seven and sixteen; to educate them in the scriptures and general knowledge, to qualify them to earn an honest livelihood, and to assist poor widows with large families of young and helpless children'. The Church of England had a strong influence on the Home and the boys were sent to church schools.

J Crone, builder c1905 at 17 Upper Lewes Road

John Cox, remembering his time at St Peter's National Boys' School in Richmond Buildings in the early 1900s, reflected that his class contained a group of boys from the Orphan Boys' Home.

Benefactors supported the orphanage and subscriptions were also sought from the public. Boys had to be nominated as suitable cases for assistance by members of the church or respected members of the public. The 1881 census shows twenty- three boys between the ages of eight and fifteen apprenticed to gas fitting, printing, carpentry and French polishing firms. In the 1891 and 1901 census there were apprentices in basket making, mechanical engineering, photography, upholstery, picture frame making and printing.

The superintendent and matron of the home were always a married couple who lived on the premises. The longest serving couple was George and Gertrude Excell who ran the home from 1910 until its closure in 1937. Mrs. Excell appears to have been superintendent and matron during the last few years before its closure, so it can be assumed that the numbers of boys in care had decreased.

Other local residents in the area can remember the boys at the home:

"There were about twelve of them and they were all orphans. They didn't wear a uniform and the younger ones attended local schools. Some of the boys were apprenticed to Mr Bourne in Park Crescent Road, who made shoes and boots as well as repairing them. The boys were trained to earn their own living when they left the home."
Eileen Gower

There were changes in attitudes and greater municipal provision for homeless children after the Second World War, and small local charity orphanages gradually closed. The house on the corner of Wakefield Road still remains today but without the boys to remind us of a different age

Shops and Traders

In 1854 there were just a few private houses at the Ditchling Road end of the present Upper Lewes Road (sometimes known as Alfred Terrace), but no shops or traders, except Arthur Rushbridge at the New Inn.

By 1867, when Caledonian, Edinburgh, Aberdeen, Inverness, Mary Magdalene and St Paul's Streets had been completed, small shops appeared on the street corners along Upper Lewes Road. In 1869 there were, amongst others, a builder, a nurseryman, a florist, a corn dealer, a dairyman, a baker and a 'rustic works'. As the area grew, so did the number and range of traders including boot makers and repairers, confectioners, potato salesmen and laundresses. By 1880 other small businesses had opened, including fly proprietors, dressmakers, a plumassier (trader in ornamental feathers, fashionable at the time), chocolate manufacturers and Tomkins & Co, tennis outfitters and racquet stringers. The shops remained on the south-east side of Upper Lewes Road whilst light industry developed on the other side.

These Upper Lewes Road shops were small and suffered from competition from the larger shops in Lewes Road, such as Home & Colonial, Maypole, Timothy Whites and the Co-op. The advantages of the corner shop were that they were local, opened for longer hours, and would deliver and particularly give credit.

Eileen Gower grew up at 119 Upper Lewes Road after the First World War and can remember the little corner shops:

"There were six children in our family, but we were better off than many others because my dad was an antique dealer and had his own shop and workshop in the town. My mother was a good dressmaker and made all our clothes, but she still had to shop carefully and daily as there were no fridges. She usually sent us kids out to shop as she was always busy working. I used to be sent to Deeprose grocer's shop at the top of St. Paul's Street to buy food. If you were 'stuck' he would book it and you could pay at the end of the week. You could take a jam jar and buy half a penny's worth of mustard pickle, jam or black treacle. Mum also used Goldring's bakery in St. Paul's Street and she took her cakes and Sunday dinners to be cooked in their ovens. My mother did use the larger shops in Lewes Road, especially Deveson's greengrocer and Pearks for dried peas. We bought 7lb of coal from Denyers, on the corner of St. Paul's Street, where you could take your own sack and the old girl would weigh it for you. I also remember second

hand furniture shops and Richards where you could buy half penny's worth of elastic and a penny-worth of ribbon."
Eileen Gower

"There were small grocers who would deliver, and a fish and chip shop, but mostly trade warehouses. We didn't know what they were because they didn't have shop windows."
Ron French

There were several boot repairers in Upper Lewes Road and in the side streets around. When Harold Bernard first moved into his shop trade was non-existent because there was already an established shoe repairer in the area. He had a friend across the road who brought all her shoes to him, he repaired them and put them on display and gradually trade picked up.

"I can go back to it being a bakers originally. There's a big oven down in the cellar, you know those ovens that are like a hole in the wall. Later it was a little grocer's shop and then a wireless shop. We moved in in 1957 and had the shop as a greengrocer, but turned it into a breakfast café, 6 am through to 2 pm. When we first opened it was all coalmen as customers; in Richmond Road there was a coal yard. Then gradually builders, roofers and casual passers-by called in. There were a lot of students towards the end as well, many of the houses starting turning into university student houses. We were ever so busy on Saturday mornings – nearly all students."
Sheila Hunt, who lived at 106 Upper Lewes Road.

Today many of the small shops have been converted to houses and those businesses remaining are architects, central heating engineers, shutters and blind suppliers, a mini supermarket, café, fish and chip shop, newsagents and a public house.

In 1862 a small terrace of houses, Ranelagh Terrace, ran from what is now Roundhill Road to Princes Road. It is now just a part of Ditchling Road and several of the houses were converted to shops. There was a grocer, a hairdresser and a bootmaker but the old grocer's shop, now Shakti's Stores, is the only one left.

"I lived in Princes Crescent in the 1930s but we didn't use the greengrocers on the corner much, his stock always looked sad and the floor of the shop unsafe. I would be sent to buy vegetables at the small nursery in Belton Road that backed onto our garden wall."
S K

"I remember the butchers (in Princes Crescent), where on Mondays in the late 20s the ice lorry would arrive and deliver loads of ice to keep the meat cool. There weren't any refrigerators then. We would always get a piece to suck when the driver wasn't looking. Then there was the grocer, who used to sell fabulous broken biscuits and, when in season, gooseberries and we'd buy one penny-worth in newspaper."

Olive Masterton

9 Princes Crescent c1950. The Crescent Hairdressers, previously a greengrocers owned by the Jennings family. Mr Jennings can be seen peeping through the window. It is now Marcia's hairdressers

There was also Clark's the bakers.

"Before that it was Gigins. It goes back almost to the building of these houses. The bakers was sold and new owners decided to have a garage built. They had to ask my permission because it came against my wall. They dug it all out and altered the front of the building – we used to have a nice curved railing which went all round. They dug out under my wall where the ovens from the bakery had been – where the people in the past had done their Sunday dinners.'

Old Age Pensioner

Other small shops opened in the side streets, some in front rooms of houses: Cyril Wood's family came to Brighton in 1932 because of his mother's poor health.

"My reactions on seeing my father's 'new' shop, at 5 Mayo Road, in Brighton for the first time were mixed. There was a sense of disbelief as I beheld not a double-fronted emporium to which I had become accustomed, but a shop in the front room of a house. The small, confined space boasted two counters, and crammed on its shelves were goods of every description. The greengrocery department consisted of tiers of boxes containing potatoes, cabbages, and carrots. There was the oil and wood section – a huge tank of paraffin operated by hand pump, and dozens of bundles of firewood stacked against the counter. Sometimes there were even 'coal' briquettes (compressed coal dust). Large blocks of cooking salt had to be cut into penny cubes, and dried fruit, cereals, rice, etc., weighed carefully into paper bags and sold for a few coppers.

Father had his own blend of tea and this, too, often passed over the counter in little 'twists' of paper at a penny a time. There was also the confectionery counter. Children on their way to school would pile into the shop to feast their eyes on the rows of bottles of sweets and chocolates – not to mention the tins of broken biscuits.

Next door to us was a large laundry and when the midday hooter sounded, and sometimes at teatime too, the girls would pour in to buy their lunchtime snacks. Often these would be capped with a penn'orth of pickles doled out by my father from a large stone jar with a wooden spoon and deposited into waiting cups. Sadly, early in 1940, whilst endeavouring to provide a service for his customers, he fell in the snow. He died a few weeks later as result of his injuries. I was just 18."

Cyril Wood

Many of the small shops in the area closed following the advent of the supermarket and the increase in traffic which made passing trade difficult. Most of the corner shops in Upper Lewes Road have now been converted to houses but some small workshops and businesses still exist on the northwest side. Some original workshop entrances can still be seen in Princes Road and Roundhill Street evoking memories of over one hundred years of trading.

Healthcare and Illness

The Roundhill district has two claims for inclusion in the annals of medical history: at the beginning of the twentieth century it housed a pioneering mental health facility, and fifty years later it found itself at the centre of a potentially serious smallpox outbreak.

Funeral 1911. The shop on the left is Walter Wood, grocer, 126 Ditchling Road

Mental Health

In 1899 a local practitioner, Doctor Helen Boyle, had set up a dispensary for women and children at 145 Islingword Road for those 'too poor to afford the usual doctor's fees.' Consultations were free but there was a threepenny charge for medicines. The dispensary was under the patronage of the Countess of Chichester.

In 1905 the dispensary was incorporated into a hospital for nervous disorders which she opened, in rented premises at 101 Roundhill Crescent. The Lewes Road Hospital and Dispensary for Women and Children had twelve beds and a cot. It was the first facility of its kind in England, set up for the early treatment of mental illness.

The nineteenth century had witnessed major changes in the treatment of the mentally ill. At the beginning of the century those afflicted had been seen as sub-human and suffered brutal treatment. They were imprisoned in madhouses, fed on a meagre diet, often cruelly restrained and, labelled incurable, were lost to society. By the middle of the century medical ideas were changing. Many believed that sufferers would benefit from treatment in a more humane institution, cocooned in a regimented but paternalistic environment, with a programme of 'suitable occupations and diversions' to enforce self-discipline and good citizenship. Consequently The Lunatics Act of 1845 had required all local authorities in England and Wales to provide asylums for the care and treatment of the mentally ill, without restraint.

In reality however asylums failed to fulfil these worthy aims; they rapidly became overcrowded, under-funded and under-staffed. Personal care and treatment deteriorated and inmates could be detained against their will. Incarceration in an asylum stigmatised the patient and it was universally dreaded.

Until the setting up of the little hospital in Roundhill Crescent the only way to obtain psychiatric help was to be admitted to an institution. Ahead of her time, Doctor Boyle believed that cases of temporary insanity could be cured if caught early enough, and certification could be avoided in the majority of cases. She understood that the mental problems of poor women were often as a result of their living conditions, malnutrition, overwork and the stresses of childbirth and motherhood. She employed only female staff so that the hospital provided treatment of women by women, which she thought essential for a sympathetic therapeutic atmosphere. After-care was provided too, and discharged patients were encouraged to return to join in hospital activities so that continuing support could be provided.

In 1910 the hospital moved to larger premises at 8 Ditchling Road, taking over adjoining houses within two years, to provide for medical and surgical cases as well. The psychiatric department moved to Brunswick Place in Hove in 1912 as expansion continued, and the Brighton and Hove branches became known collectively as The Lady Chichester Hospital after their patron.

The two units went their separate ways in 1918. Helen Boyle was adamant that treatment in the psychiatric department must continue to be free of charge and this caused a rift between them. The Brighton branch became The New Sussex Hospital and continued to treat mainly gynaecological problems. Adopted by the new National Health Service in 1948 it finally closed in 1980. The Lady Chichester Hospital continued to expand as a psychiatric unit, moving to New Church Road in 1920. From its humble beginnings in Roundhill Crescent it became a modern 70 bed National Health Service hospital, continuing to serve the community until 1988 when, in accordance with modern thinking, the inpatient facility was closed and it became a day centre for outpatients.

The Lewes Road Hospital for Women and Children had challenged accepted psychiatric practice, pioneering voluntary inpatient treatment and initiating care in the community with its continuing outpatient support. Certification is a rarity now, thanks in no small part to the example of Doctor Helen Boyle.

Diphtheria

"I suppose one of my earliest memories is being in the hospital – up at the sanatorium in Bear Road when I was about seven years old with diphtheria. In Upper Lewes Road in the 1920s they had the road up, the water was bad I think, because I got diphtheria. I know my father used to wear a white coat and he had to speak to me from outside a window. Of course we had the epidemic of influenza in 1918. That was a terrible affair. I remember the horses coming up Upper Lewes Road going to the cemetery. Horses – fine black horses they had.
My father died in 1918 of cancer. When he was buried it was four black horses and a hearse. It cost twelve shillings and six pence. Unfortunately my mother was left with four children. Many a time I had a jug of soup and a piece of bread for my dinner. There used to be a kitchen down by the market, Marshall's Row … I used to get soup there for my mother."
Ernest Austen

Scarlet Fever

"Christine started school for about three weeks and then she caught scarlet fever. When the health people came they said they weren't going to take her away, not going to take her to hospital. And I said, 'Well I don't want the baby to get it', he was only nine months old. And they said 'Well, it's the same family so it doesn't matter … you'll have to hang a white sheet at the bedroom door and dip it in disinfectant.' So I said, 'What's the good of that because we've all got to go in there to sleep tonight. Got nowhere else to sleep.' They didn't have an answer for that, so we didn't have the sheet up and Brian got scarlet fever as well."
Mrs Gausden

Pre-National Health Service

"Some streets, like St Mary Magdalene and St Paul's Street, seemed poor. There was a poor woman down St Paul's Street whose husband was a sailor and she had a load of kids. My mother took a coat out of her wardrobe,

unpicked it and made coats for the kids, and put fur on the top or bottom.
The Sisters of Mercy lived in Gladstone Terrace and dressed like nuns. If
you couldn't afford a doctor, which was 2/6d in those days, you went to the
church and got a letter and took it to the Sisters of Mercy across the road,
and they would give you a paper which said you could have a doctor for
one shilling."
Eileen Gower

Smallpox

On 27 December 1950 when Brighton was in the grip of a flu epidemic, a
young woman was admitted to Bevendean Hospital in a poor state and was
causing concern. Her father too had been detained there with similar
symptoms and died within a couple of days. Smallpox was suspected,
despite the disease having been eradicated from Britain since the 1930s.
Samples sent to the Public Health Laboratories at Colindale confirmed the
diagnosis. Brighton was now at risk of a major outbreak of one of the most
contagious diseases known to medical science.

The dead man was Harold Bath of 13 Kemp Street in the North Laine. Both
he and his daughter Elsie had recently had her Royal Air Force officer
boyfriend to stay with them. Flight Lieutenant Hunter was on leave from a
posting in India and, during his stay in Brighton had been constantly unwell.
They had assumed it was a recurrent bout of malaria, but he had recovered
and gone to join his squadron in Scotland.

On 29 December a public health emergency was declared. The Medical
Officer of Health for Brighton, Doctor Rutherford Cramb and his team
located the airman and immediately sent him with Elsie for isolation in the
smallpox hospital at Dartford. The military authorities were notified and
several thousand RAF personnel were vaccinated. In Brighton, Harold
Bath's contacts were traced, as the Ministry of Health explained later:

> 'On the morning of 29 December we had traced his taxi. We
> disinfected it, and had the relief driver vaccinated and placed
> under observation. Then we started to trace some of the people
> who had ridden in the taxi. The result was, I had to notify
> Medical Officers in Devonshire, Kent, Lancashire, Scotland and
> Northern Ireland."
> **Brighton and Hove Herald 10 February 1951**

Elsie Bath herself was a telephonist at the Brighton Telephone Exchange.
On the same day another team of health inspectors visited the premises and

the entire staff was vaccinated, but they chose not to fumigate the premises as they did not want to have to shut it down, because in the event of a major epidemic an efficient telephone system would be vital. However ten days later another telephonist contracted smallpox, so fumigation had to be carried out. The exchange did not cease to function though,

> 'While the interior was full of dense fumes the exchange carried on, manned by the telephone manager, Mr L Hill, the exchange superintendent, Mr P M Reekie and the chief supervisor Mr Latter, all wearing Civil Defence gas respirators.'

Brighton & Hove Herald 20 January 1951

Tivoli Laundry c1920, owned by the Bowden family of Crescent Road

On the 30 and 31 December two new cases were admitted to hospital. They both worked at the Tivoli Laundry in Crescent Road, Roundhill. Every week Harold and Elsie Bath sent their dirty linen there and this had infected the women who sorted the laundry, other employees subsequently became ill too. Although the laundry was not closed down by the authorities, in early January the managing director Mr F C Bowden was forced to send customers the following letter:

'Dear Sir or Madam,

It is with sincere regret that we have to inform you of a serious delay in our service to you. At the closing of the old year fate dealt us a blow in connection with the outbreak of smallpox. Several members of our staff have fallen victims and as a precautionary measure the remainder of the staff, who are all quite well, have been stood off from work for a fortnight.

The Ministry of Health authorities have been in constant touch with us since the commencement of the outbreak, and we are abiding by their instructions in all that we do. They called on customers where it was found necessary to do so, informing them as to what action to take. Our works and vans have been fumigated twice by them.

The staff who are not affected worked gallantly last week in an effort to cope with the situation, but due to the absence of the experienced checkers and packers the task became impossible. It is, therefore, with great reluctance that we have to inform you that our usual collections and deliveries will be suspended for two weeks, that is until week commencing 22 January.'

Brighton & Hove Herald 13 January 1951

Later the local paper related a 'macabre incident at midnight' in a laundry,

'After a woman patient had been removed to hospital, the Health Department found that her washing had been sent to a large laundry with more than 4,000 customers. It was 10 o'clock at night and the proprietor lived outside Brighton. Dr Cramb telephoned him and got the address of his manageress in Brighton.

Having obtained the key from her, Dr Rutherford Cramb himself and four health inspectors went to the laundry, put on protective gowns and gloves and started searching among the bundles of washing. They found it about midnight. Fortunately, it had not been unwrapped, otherwise the circle of contacts might have been enlarged by several thousands.'

Brighton & Hove Herald 10 February 1951

The Tivoli was not the only establishment to be badly affected by the outbreak. Immediately after the death of Harold Bath, Bevendean Hospital had been placed in quarantine; the staff and patients were locked in for thirty-four days and all supplies had to be delivered outside the gates to reduce the risk of the spread of infection. New cases were then sent to Dartford Isolation Hospital and later, because of the icy conditions that winter, to Foredown Hospital in Portslade, though it too was undergoing stringent quarantine measures. Several of the staff at Bevendean Hospital contracted the disease, reported in the local press:

> 'One of the most alarming and tragic features of the outbreak is that three nurses and two domestic workers from Bevendean Hospital, where a woman patient was taken before if was realised that she was suffering from smallpox, have died, while several more members of the staff, including other nurses, have been affected.
>
> Another particularly tragic death was that of Miss Pamela Moreby of Brewer Street, an 18-year-old probationer nurse who died on Thursday. A girl of deeply religious convictions, she had adopted nursing from a sense of vocation, and only started at Bevendean on 18 December.'

Brighton & Hove Herald 13 January 1951

A jobbing gardener employed at the hospital also contracted smallpox and died, his only contact with the patients being when he entered the building to remove the Christmas tree on Twelfth Night.

As well as dealing with those directly affected it was necessary to protect the rest of the population. Winifred Patchin, a Roundhill resident, remembers,

"There was panic because so many Brighton people were vaccinated."
Maud Gill explained her role:

"What they asked the Community Nurses to do was to help doctors at the surgeries. So we helped with the patients. The doctors gave the treatment but we helped write their names down and did the dressing on them. But it all went very smoothly and in one afternoon we got through many people."
Many were vaccinated on their employers' insistence; they would not be allowed to work without it.

"At work at Allen West's we all had to have a jab."
Harold Ansell

However the treatment often had unpleasant consequences and many working days were lost as a result. In fact, for some the after-effects of the jab were quite disagreeable. Bruce Avis, a teacher living in Crescent Road, recalled:

"I came home from school one day to see my parents looking very dejected because there was an outbreak of smallpox from the laundry. (One of the ladies who worked there) was seriously ill and my father (a builder and

decorator) had been working there and the Public Health Authority came to
see my parents and told them they'd both got to be vaccinated against
smallpox. I did have two miserable parents! They went to bed; they were
quite ill for a bit because they weren't youngsters!'

At last, however, on the 6 February, the 'all clear' signal was given by the
Health Department, as there had been no new cases for fourteen days. The
outbreak had been successfully contained within Brighton, more than 70,000
people had been vaccinated in less than a month and about 14,000 suspected
contacts were traced. In all thirty-five people caught the disease, ten died,
six were employees of Bevendean Hospital and two, Ethel Brooks and Mrs
E Connor, worked at the Tivoli Laundry.

The mobilisation of public health workers had been phenomenally efficient
and successful: 15,000 contacts were traced and 92,000 people were
vaccinated. On 10 February the Brighton and Hove Herald paid tribute to all
involved by listing those who deserved praise for their efforts:

> 'Doctor Rutherford Cramb the Medical Officer of Health who
> remained imperturbable but swift in decision throughout the
> crisis.
>
> Mr W S Parker the indefatigable Deputy Medical Officer of
> Health
>
> Mr Robert S Cross, the Chief Health Inspector, and his assistants
> who worked ceaselessly for five weeks, tracing contacts and
> destroying infected materials.
>
> The medical, nursing and domestic staffs of the Bevendean and
> Foredown hospitals.
>
> Doctors and nurses who staffed the vaccination centres.
>
> General practitioners who provided vaccination for thousands at
> their surgeries, in many instances not bothering to claim the 'fees'
> to which they were entitled.
>
> The ambulance drivers of the Health Department. Members of the
> Women's Voluntary Service and all helpers.'

It is worth noting that this was not the first instance of effective prophylactic
treatment for an outbreak of smallpox in Brighton. Nearly two hundred
years before a previous outbreak had given the opportunity for one of the
earliest examples of mass vaccination. In 1786 a smallpox epidemic in the
town was countered by the vaccination nearly one thousand nine hundred
people at a cost of two shillings and sixpence for poorer people and seven
shillings and sixpence for the wealthy. The results were not quite as good as
in 1951 but still saved the lives of a lot of Brighton people.

Roundhill at War

Brighton was not an important target for enemy bombing during the Second World War.

"We weren't expecting to be bombed. When the planes flew over towards London, the barrage was so great they turned round and flew back. When they could see the sea they just dropped the bombs because they knew that there would be houses somewhere along the coast. That's how Brighton got these odd bombs."
Bruce Avis

Nevertheless between 15 July 1940 and 22 March 1944 Brighton suffered 56 air attacks, 198 people lost their lives and many more were injured or rendered homeless.

The Roundhill area itself incurred no direct hits but there were some close calls. The first of these was on 20 September 1940, the target probably being the Lewes Road railway viaduct.

> 'The raider hovered over a thickly populated working-class district and dropped two screaming bombs. Each scored a direct hit, one striking a group of workmen's houses and the other the Franklin Arms in Lewes Road.'
> **The Evening Argus 21 September 1940**

Ernest Austin, who had spent his childhood living opposite the Martha Gunn, then the New Inn, knew the area well and was, by then, working as a fitter for the Gas Company. He had a narrow escape that day.

"I went to this place in Caledonian Road and borrowed a pair of steps from the girl who lived there to connect the meter up. I went to Hartington Road and while there a bomb drops on this house I've been in, and the steps were blown up through the roof."
Ernest Austin

"The bomb didn't just destroy the pub, it destroyed the greengrocers next door and the wool shop called Platts Martin next door to that. Platts Martin did reopen again, the rest didn't. My mother had just left to go down to Lewes Road for some shopping, and I was looking out of the back window of the house in Roundhill Crescent. The window had been taped up, criss-cross fashion, to restrict the damage that could be caused by bomb blast. I spotted a yellow plane, I recognised it as a Heinkel. It swooped down and appeared to be coming straight for us. When the bomb came out of the

plane Lewes Road exploded. The plane swooped over the house, towards Ditchling Road. The window I was looking out of fell into the room, but the glass remained intact. The plane continued to machine gun the area, and the houses in Princes Crescent had bullet holes on their garden walls for some time."
Peter Foreman

Wartime was not always so exciting or alarming. Fire-watching was a dull nightly pursuit, as Doreen Blake remembers:

"I did my fire watching duties for the Royal Engineers' Record Office, now the Brighton Business Centre, at Hill Lodge. Rosters were printed and circulated and when your name appeared you did your duty, which lasted all night. We had all been trained to deal with incendiary bombs and when the air raid warning sounded, the men watched outside while we women watched from the upstairs windows. It was rather eerie, especially if it was a wild and windy night, with the trees in the grounds making a noise with the swaying branches.
We had our share of scares too, when the 'Tip and Run' raiders would fly in low over the sea, drop their bombs, then head off. One day … I heard what I thought was coke being delivered out in the yard to stoke up the boilers. Suddenly somebody shouted 'Get down', Get down', so I immediately dropped to the floor. Then I learned we were being machine gunned and our building was peppered with bullets. What a blessing our walls were so thick. Another time a bomb ricocheted off our roof, straight into a row of little houses in Rose Hill Terrace, destroying the lot and killing a number of people. My poor mother suffered the tortures of the damned as rumours flew around that the College had received a direct hit."
War brought other concerns to Doreen in the Record Office post room.

"All went well until Dunkirk when sack upon sack filled the post room. Most mail had been damaged, the contents spilling out, which had us in tears as locks of hair, rosary beads, photographs, letters, birthday cards, prayer books and poems fell out – such intimate things for strangers to see. The worst part was when the Part 2 Orders listed the men who were 'Killed in Action', or 'Missing in Action' or 'Missing Presumed Dead'."
Doreen Blake

Street Life

"Mr Christmas, who lived along the road, had a long white beard. My grandfather who was visiting had a portable radio in the house and he asked Mr Christmas to come and look at it. Mr Christmas listened to the news … Then he shouted 'Tis the work of the Devil'… and stormed out."
Bruce Avis

"I was born at 50 Roundhill Crescent in 1935, but the family moved to no 52. My father hired a hand cart and we did the move ourselves over the course of the day. All the milk, bread and coal were delivered to the door by horse and cart. My father had the first car in the street early in 1950."
Peter Foreman

The Salvation Army

"When I was young the Salvation Army used to come along the road every Sunday morning. There was a lady called Mrs Carter, she was a Salvationist – they used to play outside her house every Sunday morning because she wasn't able to get there. They came along Upper Lewes Road, down St Paul's Street, along Park Crescent Road and back through Park Crescent,"
Joyce Poole

"The Salvation Army used to come up every Sunday morning, and they'd play their music. Nearly every other house in Princes Road had Salvation Army people in it. I don't know why they all came and lived there- perhaps because they were near the Congress Hall."
Mrs Gausden

Sunday School

"St Martin's Sunday School had processions around the streets and you would see the children all dressed up in their best clothes. They would go along Wellington Road and down Franklin Road and back to the church."
Mrs C.

Cat creep

"Of course I used to play in the streets, Roundhill Crescent, all up and down the cats' creep, Lennox Road, that's what it's called, isn't it? It was 1912 I think - we were at Ashdown Road. We would play in the streets around there, no traffic in those days. You had to be really well off to own a car then. In those days you didn't worry where the children went. Princes Road, 'Steep Princes' we used to call it, and in the winter time we used to

get a tray, not on the side where the houses are, but the other side - the
railway side - and shoot right down there. Of course you had to walk up
again."
Mrs Clarke

"We always used to take the short cut down the cats' creep. It's in a dreadful
condition now, isn't it? It was a relatively safe place then. I wouldn't go
there now. At the bottom of the cats' creep, on the opposite corner, there's a
big house with lions over the door. My friend used to live in there. I would
go and visit her, and we used to go up all the 108 steps – and I used to
hump a pram up with one baby in it, and trailing the other one behind."
Mrs Gausden

"The cats' creep was frequented by an eccentric called Charlie who would
recite Shakespeare to the children – a harmless itinerant."
Ron Burleton

"When I was in my teens my friend lived in St Paul's Street and I would use
the cats' creep as a short cut from Princes Crescent. As I got older I would
stay out later and it would be dark when I made my way home. I was rather
nervous of going up it in the dark, but the alternative was a long walk and
being late home. I was fit then because I could run from bottom to top
without stopping. I couldn't do it now."
J C

From Ruby Goodall's diary of 1910-12 when she was a student teacher in
Brighton:

> 'Walked to Rottingdean – there met 'The Two' – Oh the giddy
> socks. Walked home in couples… Lost ourselves in the by-streets
> off Lewes Road and - Oh the cat's creek (sic) steps. Arrived home
> very tired at 10.15 pm after worrying the kind friends of '55'
> [Princes Crescent].'
> **Wednesday 21 June 1911**

The lamplighter, the muffin man and the milkman

"We used to play in the street quite a lot. We had a double fronted house,
two front doors together, which left a foot of tiled square area which we
used to play on when we weren't belting up and down the road on our
scooters wearing the heels of our shoes out. Almost opposite us was a street
lamp and I remember the lamplighter coming up with his short ladder and
his hooked pole to switch on what would have been gas lamps. He used to
come along and switch those on at night and switch them off again in the

74

morning. Of course on Sunday the muffin man used to come around with his tray on his head covered with baize, and the winkle man with his two-wheeled cart selling his half pints of winkles. The milkman used to come with the old pram with a churn on it."
Winifred Patchin

Cinemas

"The Gaiety cinema was pulled down when they built Sainsbury's. It was a lovely cinema there, built in 1939; it was art deco. There was another cinema in Lewes Road called the Arcadia. That's where the Labour Club is now."
Joyce Poole

"Cinema – used to get to go twice a week. They used to change the programme Wednesday and Saturday. Then there was the old Arcadia cinema, used to go in there for a penny every Saturday afternoon."
Ernest Austen

"There was a cinema called 'The Gaiety'. Then the road that goes by Sainsburys didn't exist. You went into the Gaiety next to the pub and walked through a long corridor because the cinema was at the back where Sainsburys is now."
Bruce Avis

Trams

"I remember the trams, they never had any covering over the top deck; all you would get was a little mackintosh to put over the knees. I remember the solid tyre buses – go over a bump and you would know all about it. I used to ride a bike for 30 years and if I got on the tram lines over I went."
Ernest Austen.

Play

"In the mid-1940s Wakefield Road was a haven for children with virtually no traffic to interrupt our play. The flint wall opposite number 14 had a chalk wicket drawn on it for summer cricket and chalk goalposts for winter football. Occasionally we would have to stop our games to allow the milk cart and baker's cart to make their deliveries and once a week in winter the coal cart would come round. Any manure dropped by the horses was scooped up in a flash by the residents. A motorcar was a rare sight indeed!"
Colin Mather

Public Houses

There used to be three public houses in the Conservation Area but nowadays there are only two: the 'Round Hill' and the 'New Vic'. The missing one is the 'Duke of Wellington' which from 1860 to around 1910 stood in Rose Hill at number seven. It was plainly an ale house converted from a private house. Today its site lies under the south end of the block of flats in Rose Hill, built in place of the bomb-damaged cottages after the War.

Both of the remaining two were originally tied houses of Tamplin's Brewery. In the mid 1990s, the 'Round Hill' became a free house, whilst the 'New Vic' passed initially to Courage Brewery, and thereafter became a free house owned by group called Punch Taverns.

The 'Round Hill' building dates from 1868; plans show three bars and five bedrooms, but it is not shown as trading until 1877, with George Willard as the first publican. The building has changed little over time, except that a single bar has replaced the separate Public, Saloon, Private, and the 'Bottle and Jug' bars.

The 'Victoria Inn' in Richmond Road was not listed in the street directories as a building until the mid 1880s, when it took the number 31a, suggesting it was inserted between other buildings in the street. This building, perhaps a temporary structure, was originally a greengrocer, but this ceased trading in 1889, and two years later was listed as a public house. The building has Edwardian pargetting and is slightly out of context with nearby buildings.

Just outside the Conservation Area are four other public houses. The 'Jolly Brewer' actually started life as the 'Jolly Huntsman', the name connecting it of the dog kennels of the Brighton Harriers which were nearby in what was Dog Kennel Road. The building is of the florid classic late Victorian style which is in sharp contrast to the adjacent small cottages.

'The Bugle' in St Martin's Street is tucked away off the main road and has a reputation as a welcoming local which firmly retains its Victorian character.

The road that was to become the Upper Lewes Road was previously called Gypsy Lane because it was the route of gypsies who wintered every year near the 'Bear Inn' at the foot of Bear Road, where there was a dew pond for water and was near the town for work and provisions.

The 'New Inn' in Upper Lewes Road was first listed in 1862. The first publican was Arthur Rushbridge. The name of the pub was changed to the

Martha Gunn in 1973 when public houses that could not offer accommodation were not allowed to be called 'Inns'. It took the name of a famous Brighton Victorian sea bathing attendant, Martha Gunn, though the area does not appear to have a connection with that activity, or with the woman herself.

Victoria Inn 31a Richmond Road c1915, built in 1898, now called the Queen Vic. The first four tenants were women

Endpiece

It was a big day back in 1989 when they started to pull down the old Cox's Pill Factory. On the corner of the Lewes Road knots of people stood and stared.

There were mums and dads, children and grandparents. Some of them had worked in the factory and were there to tell the tale. Linked across the generations, what was witnessed was more than just the destruction of another brick in the wall of the Roundhill community.

Today there seems little left to distinguish Roundhill from the rest. Inside the triangle though, you can still see a path that leads back over two hundred years. This book has been the story of that path and the signposts along the way.

If the area was a series of picture postcards taken over time, there would be one message at the centre of a mantelpiece full of memories. It's a scene with a small girl, it must be around the turn of the nineteenth century. She is playing count the cat creep steps as she skips one early morning to a new elementary school. On one side, down a curving crescent, are nurseries and small holdings and on the other side, workmens' yards. There, with a windmill as a backdrop, forever in a frame, is the story of the Roundhill community.

Communities live on not just in memory and local history books. They live on in the dreams, aspirations, hopes and fears and trials and tribulations of a new generation and then the next.

Cox's Pill Factory has been replaced by a Sainsbury's supermarket. One moving tribute remains. It's the old clock, set back up high in the brickwork. Cleaned up, with a new mechanism and freshly painted numbers, it stands there still. Slowly and silently, in rhythmic motion, just as much a testament as a timepiece, it looks down at the changing scene. Today, as it did yesterday, it tells us the time and marks each moment as it passes.

The Round Hill Society

The Society was formed in 1999. Its aim is to create a sense of community and to protect the environmental interests of the area. It addresses issues such as traffic problems, street cleanliness and conservation, and has received grants to buy equipment and hold events such as street and garden parties. Each December it holds a 'Carols and Candles' procession around our local streets, finishing with mulled wine and mince pies. Public meetings, on topics such as local history, urban wildlife etc are popular.

Round Hill Local History Group

At the first Annual General Meeting of the Society, Jacqueline Pollard, a local historian, gave an illustrated talk on the history of the Round Hill area. This prompted some members of the Society to set up of a History Group, and the momentum to do so increased when the Group acquired some archive papers relating to the area.

Initially the Group was involved in transcribing these documents to gain an insight into the background of the development of the area and, from this beginning, it was decided to interview some of the long-standing residents and ex-residents to gather their memories of the district. It was intended to print some of these recollections in the Round Hill Reporter, the community news sheet, but the project developed instead into the proposal for a book from the material collected.

The Group has extended its remit beyond the current Conservation Area to include the whole of the geographical area of historical Roundhill.

This publication is the culmination of the Group's efforts to bring to the current residents of Round Hill a feel for its past. Meanwhile enjoy the book and walk around the area with new eyes.

Group members:

Pam Blackman. Katherine Crossley, Rosemary Fittock, Peggy Henderson, Lindsey Lee, Lucy O'Shea, William Parker, Andrew Partington, Jenn Price, Marigold Rogers, Ann Stutfield, Diana Truscott, Jacqueline Pollard and Chris Tullett.

Contributors

Historical and picture research sponsored by Leslie Wilmot

E A, Brenda Ashong, Harold Ansell, Ernest Austen, Bruce Avis, Sue Banks, Roger Barker, Doreen Blake, Brighton & Hove City Council: Draft Round Hill Character Statement, Alex Brown, Harry Bull, Ron Burleton, J C, Carol, Mrs C, Mrs Clarke, Jan Curry, Simeon Elliott, Peter Foreman, Connie French, Ron French, Mrs. Gausden, Maud Gill, Eileen Gower, Tom Gower, Peggy Henderson, Anne Hill, Sheila Hunt, S K, Diana Knapp, Lyn Mansfield-Osbourne, Colin Mather, Geoff Mead, Ann Nealer, Winifred Patchin, Sylvia Pawlowstia, Barbara Petrarca, Joyce Poole, Gladys Prevett, Jenn Price, Jessie Robinson, Allie Rogers, Marigold Rogers, Susie Sharp, Valerie Slade, Donald & Shelagh Winter, Cyril Wood, Christine Zaniewicka and other Roundhill residents

Design, editing and proof reading:

Editing and design: Selma Montford. Research, editing and proof reading: Derek Burns Assistance: Peter Booth. Section introductions: Simon Montgomery

Maps: East Sussex Record Office

Photographs and prints

Doreen Blake, Peter Booth, John Coleman, Barry Eliades, Martin Hayes: West Sussex County Library Service, Worthing Library; J S Gray collection: courtesy of the Regency Society of Brighton & Hove, Chris Horlock, Diana Knapp, Geoff Mead, Selma Montford, Jacqueline Pollard, Rob Sanderson of Talbot Photography, Rob Stephenson, Vanessa Sykes and Phillip Wood

Picture and historical research, and interviews:

Jacqueline Pollard and members of the Roundhill Local History Group

Bibliography

'Brighton Behind the Front', QueenSpark & Lewis Cohen Urban Studies Centre at Brighton Polytechnic, No 24, ISBN No. 0-904733-40-8

'The Circle of Life' by Olive Masterson, (1986), QueenSpark Books,
ISBN No. 0-904733-14-9

'The Female Malady: Women, Madness and English Culture, 1830-1980', Elaine Showalter, (1985), Virago

'Hunting in the Neighbourhood' by Alderman Henry Martin, (1871). Publisher unknown

'The Kemp Town Branch Line' by Peter A. Harding, (1999), Publisher Peter Harding

'A Quiet Revolution in Brighton, Dr Helen Boyle's Pioneering Approach to Mental Health Care, 1899-1939', Louise Westwood in the 'Journal of the Society for the Social History of Medicine', (2001)

'Round Hill', Draft Conservation Area Statement, Brighton & Hove City Council, (2004)

'Secrets of the 43 Club' by Mrs Kate Meyrick (1994), Parkgate Publication Ltd.,
ISBN No 0-9523109-2-9

'Sussex Disasters', pp. 89-96, ch. City of Frightened People', W. H. Johnson, (1998),
SB Publications

'The Windmills and Millers of Brighton' by H. T. Dawes, Sussex Industrial History No 18, (1988), ISSN 0263-5151. Lewis Cohen Urban Studies Centre at the University of Brighton for the Sussex Industrial Archaeology Society

'The Jews of Brighton', The Jewish Historical Society of England Transactions – Sessions 1968-1969, volume XXII

'Pills and Pharmaceuticals, A. H. Cox and Co. Ltd., 1839-1989' by J. A. Slimm

Brighton Books (Publishing), 10 Clermont Road, Brighton BN1 6SG UK
email: brighton-books@pobox.com, phone: 01273-509209 fax: 01273-502018
Brighton Books (Publishing) have published the following books about the local area.
no 1: 'The Vanishing Villas of Preston & Withdean' by Selma Montford, Jacqueline Pollard and Robert Sanderson, (1996). ISBN No. 1-901454-00-2 @ £5.50.
no 2: 'Dr Brighton's Indian Patients' by Joyce Collins, (1997), ISBN No. 1-901454-01-0 @ £5.50.
no 4: 'Little to Spare and Nothing to Waste: a Brighton Boyhood in the Hungry Thirties' by Robert Haywood, (1998), ISBN No. 1-901454-03-7 @ £5.50.
no 6; 'Memories and Photographs of Brighton in the 20s & 30s' by H. T. Dawes, (2002), ISBN No. 1-901454-05-3 @ £6.99
no 7: 'Churchill Square Revisited : a lost Brighton community' by Andrew Walker, (2002), ISBN No. 1-901454-06-1 @ £6.99

O)her books distributed by Brighton Books (Publishing)

'Blighty Brighton: photographs and memories of Brighton in the First World War', (1991), Published by the Lewis Cohen Urban Studies Centre at Brighton Polytechnic and QueenSpark Books, ISBN No. 0-904733-55-6 @ £4.95
'Past & Present: the story of Blaker's Park', (1993), Published by the Friends of Blakers Park, ISBN No. 0-9522856-0-6 @ £5.00
'Preston: Downland Village to Brighton Suburb', (2004), Published by the Preston Village Millennium Project in association with Brighton Books (Publishing)
ISBN No. 1-901454-07-X @ £9.99
Please add £2.00 per book, £3.00 for 2 or more books for post & packing, and make the cheque payable to: Brighton Books (Publishing).

Printed by Delta Press, 2 Goldstone Street, Hove BN3 3RJ